How to Communicate
Velcro Truth in a Teflon World

D0040437

TRUTH THAT STICKS

AVERY T. WILLIS JR.
AND
MARK SNOWDEN

NAVPRESS
Discipleship Inside Out™

Discipleship Inside Out™

NavPress is the publishing ministry of The Navigators, an international Christian organization and leader in personal spiritual development. NavPress is committed to helping people grow spiritually and enjoy lives of meaning and hope through personal and group resources that are biblically rooted, culturally relevant, and highly practical.

For a free catalog go to www.NavPress.com
or call 1.800.366.7788 in the United States or 1.800.839.4769 in Canada.

ISBN-13: 978-1-61521-531-7

Cover design by Arvid Wallen

Some of the anecdotal illustrations in this book are true to life and are included with the permission of the persons involved. All other illustrations are composites of real situations, and any resemblance to people living or dead is coincidental.

Unless otherwise identified, all Scripture quotations in this publication are taken from the *Holy Bible, New International Version*® (NIV®). Copyright © 1973, 1978, 1984 by International Bible Society. Used by permission of Zondervan. All rights reserved. Other versions used include: the Holman Christian Standard Bible ® (HCSB) Copyright © 2003, 2002, 2000, 1999 by Holman Bible Publishers. Used by permission. All rights reserved; the *Holy Bible*, New Living Translation (NLT), copyright © 1996, 2004. Used by permission of Tyndale House Publishers, Inc., Wheaton, Illinois 60189. All rights reserved; and the King James Version (KJV).

Library of Congress Cataloging-in-Publication Data

Willis, Avery T.
  Truth that sticks : communicating velcro truth in a teflon world / Avery T. Willis Jr., Mark Snowden.
    p. cm.
  Includes bibliographical references.
  ISBN 978-1-61521-531-7
  1. Communication--Religious aspects--Christianity. 2. Literacy--Religious aspects--Christianity. 3. Evangelistic work. 4. Discipling (Christianity) 5. Literacy--United States. I. Snowden, Mark. II. Title.
  BV4319.W55 2010
  261.5'2--dc22

                                2010006517

Printed in the United States of America

2 3 4 5 6 7 8 / 15 14 13 12 11

"Sharing the gospel through oral and visual is the most powerful means of communication that we have available today. *Truth That Sticks* combines these great tools with methods of discipling that are fresh and effective. When you tell the gospel through a story, you never forget it, and neither will those you are discipling. Get this book now!"

—PAUL ESHLEMAN, vice president, Campus Crusade for Christ International

"From childhood to adulthood, we are all fascinated with the power of a good story. In *Truth That Sticks*, Avery Willis and Mark Snowden remind us of the power held within the stories of God's inerrant Word. With a winsome spirit, they give a wonderful defense for the use of biblical storying as a powerful means of disciple making."

—ED STETZER, president, LifeWay Research, www.edstetzer.com

"Avery Willis has been an inspiration and source of wisdom for me in understanding how to communicate with Americans who prefer to learn by visual and oral means. As I applied some of the principles Avery teaches, I discovered more effective ways to communicate biblical truths to college students."

—STEVE DOUGLASS, president, Campus Crusade for Christ International

"Why build rectangular church buildings for people who live in round huts? For generations, we have forced oral learners to step into our literate world in order to be evangelized and discipled. If you want to learn to communicate effectively with two-thirds of the world's population, you must read *Truth That Sticks*."

—DR. GORDON FORT, vice president, Global Strategy,
International Mission Board, Southern Baptist Convention

"In *Truth That Sticks*, Avery Willis and Mark Snowden share practical and proven principles about making disciples and completing the Great Commission. This book is a must-read for every leader, every Christ follower, who truly wants to be effective and make a difference."

—STEVE MOORE, president/CEO, The Mission Exchange (formerly EFMA),
www.TheMissionExchange.org

"In *Truth That Sticks*, Avery Willis and Mark Snowden have packaged all the essential reasons and examples for why and how America needs to start to tell The Story. For those who have long wondered why the people they tried to disciple seemed to grasp very little and remember even less, *Truth That Sticks* presents the tools needed to engage in powerful and reproducible methods of disciple making that everyone can use. The methods are biblically timeless and tested in today's changing cultures."

—REV. CAESAR KALINOWSKI, pastor, Soma Communities,
Tacoma, Washington

"*Truth That Sticks* is a timely book for our generation. Communicating the power of the never-changing gospel is our primary mandate. Avery and Mark have captured the power and practice of making the Word come to life through Bible storying to reach, transform, and disciple our generation. I highly recommend it."

—NANCY WILSON, global ambassador and spokesperson, StoryRunners

"*Truth That Sticks* is a timely book that addresses in a masterful manner the crucial need of discipling oral-preference learners. In addition to making an indisputable case for the existence of significant segments of the American population who prefer oral and visual means of communication, Avery Willis and Mark Snowden share valuable principles, insights, and examples related to the utilization of carefully selected Bible stories to communicate God's truth and transform lives. With great enthusiasm and a sense of urgency, I recommend this book (which comes from the hearts of two of God's choicest missionaries) to everyone who has a passion for discipling those not being reached with current methodologies."

—DR. DANIEL SANCHEZ, professor of missions,
Southwestern Baptist Theological Seminary

"This book is the most important, practical how-to book written to date on the subject of oral communication of the gospel. It is very readable, gives tremendous insight into how to develop a storying model, and answers many of the questions and criticisms of those trained in more literate forms of communication. Written by Avery Willis and Mark Snowden, two of the masters of this craft, this timely book will benefit every Christ follower from layperson to preacher."

—REV. TIM AHLEN, executive director, Great Commission Initiatives;
senior pastor, Forest Meadow Baptist Church, Dallas, Texas

"Avery Willis and Mark Snowden have ably defined the next step for Bible storying. *Truth That Sticks* is not so much a how-to text as a why-not argument for applying the already successful Bible-storying methodology to the task of discipling new believers. Their book, based on Willis's long experience with discipling and more recent growing experience with storying, defines Bible-storying discipleship as biblical, practical, proven, and challenging for today's church leadership. Sidebars and case study references by Snowden aptly illustrate how and where small-group discipling has already made a significant difference in growing churches. The authors remind us that if left undiscipled, complacent Christians will remain inactive in exercising their faith and ministry and will be in danger of falling away from a life of witness and ministry."

—J. O. TERRY, Bible-storying pioneer, International Mission Board,
Southern Baptist Convention

"It is very encouraging to hear that Avery and Mark now focus on oral realities within the United States. This book takes on a daunting task, that of rolling back the Teflon-like ignorance concerning oral needs and issues within the United States and the West while trying to make the Velcro truth concerning the oldest of human and the most common of Christ's teaching modes, that of storying, stick to the point of being commonly embraced and used in making disciples. They have on their side the stickability of stories, especially biblical stories empowered by the Holy Spirit."

—DR. JAMES B. SLACK, Bible-storying pioneer, church planting movement assessor, International Mission Board, Southern Baptist Convention

"I have had the privilege of knowing and working with both Avery and Mark for many years. Both men have been greatly used by the Lord because they are lifelong learners who are faithful to practice and pass on what the Lord is teaching them. This wonderful book is a simple and practical guide to deep and powerful truths they have gleaned over a lifetime of increasingly fruitful ministry. At e3 we are employing these approaches with great effect overseas. With this book, these approaches are now accessible for those living for the kingdom in the United States as well."

—DR. CURTIS SERGEANT, vice president, e3 International, e3 Partners Ministry

"Innovation that results in dynamic life change will be the result of those who read and use the principles of *Truth That Sticks*. What appears an innovative way to mentor others is really a return to what Jesus did: tell stories. Storytelling is part of successful communication in the world today. As we tell the story of Jesus, let's tell it in a way that sticks! Avery Willis and Mark Snowden will show you how to do it in this book. Get it. Use it. Share it with others!"

—RONNIE FLOYD, pastor, First Baptist Church, Springdale, Arkansas, and Pinnacle Hills Church, Rogers, Arkansas

"Communication is not just a keyword in marriage; it is a keyword in presenting truth that we hope will stick. It has often been said that it doesn't matter what you say if the people you are speaking to don't get it. In Avery and Mark's new book, you will learn some important principles and truths that are shaping this country, and literally the world, as it pertains to storytelling. Jesus was a master at telling stories. Let's learn from Him and from these two men."

—DR. JOHNNY HUNT, pastor, First Baptist Church, Woodstock, Georgia; president, Southern Baptist Convention

"This book is Avery Willis at his best and the gospel at its clearest! Every Great Commission Christian should do what I am doing by reading this book and giving five copies to Great Commission leaders!"

—DR. BOBBY H. WELCH, strategist for global evangelical relations, Southern Baptist Convention

"If you keep thinking what you've always thought, you'll keep getting what you've always got. When it comes to communicating the gospel and making disciples, we need to think differently. *Truth That Sticks* helps us do that. Providing practical help and using proven strategies, it is a must-read for those serious about fulfilling the Great Commission."

—DR. TOM BILLINGS, executive director, Union Baptist Association, Houston, Texas

"Sometimes the greatest story ever told can be the most difficult to tell. But *Truth That Sticks* gives us a proven, time-tested approach to communicating God's Word. This isn't just a strategy for reaching illiterate people; it's the key to reaching a whole generation that absorbs more from storytelling and media than they'll ever learn from a textbook approach."

—BEN ARMENT, director, STORY conference

"Avery Willis is a pioneer and innovator helping ministry leaders understand how to communicate the gospel in a culture of change. In *Truth That Sticks*, Mark and Avery provide a practical pathway for relevant communication in today's visual story-centered world."

—MICHAEL NOVELLI, author of *Shaped by the Story*

"Stories have power. They grab the imagination. They are readily repeated. Jesus used them constantly to convey truth to people. This book about multiplying small groups of disciples using Bible storying transforms the way we communicate our faith. Essential reading for anyone with a passion to make and train disciples, not just of oral learners in other nations but also of a generation here in the West that prefers movies to books."

—DR. FELICITY DALE, house church leader;
author of *An Army of Ordinary People*

"Fresh, informative, and critically important. Anyone who wants to be an effective communicator in the twenty-first century must understand these truths."

—REV. MARK ANDERSON, international director,
Youth With A Mission; president, Global Pastors Network/Call2All

"The question is actually very simple. Do we want to effectively communicate the gospel with most of the world? If our answer is yes, then we must embrace the clear teaching of this book. Avery Willis and Mark Snowden unlock for us the secret to effective evangelism and discipleship by the oral transmission of God's Word."

—TOM ELLIFF, senior vice president for spiritual nurture and church relations,
International Mission Board, Southern Baptist Convention

"The communication and reading patterns of the modern world have opened up new opportunities for the people of God to share the Christian message in North America as well as around the globe. This significant shift in our world should cause all of us to pause and ask serious questions regarding the methods that have historically been employed to communicate the truths of the Christian faith. Avery Willis and Mark Snowden, building on their years of experience in various cultural settings, have combined to offer a well-informed, well-presented, and creative approach to doing evangelism and disciple making through Bible storying for oral-preference learners in North America. While some will continue to contend for more traditional approaches, *Truth That Sticks* is worthy of our serious reflection as we look for strategic ways to engage the world missionally with the good news of the gospel."

—DR. DAVID DOCKERY, president, Union University, Jackson, Tennessee

"The content presented in this book sets a blaze that will disciple thousands who learn only from 'sensory learning loops.' It is obvious this method is needed in the Western world. Read this book with a highlighter in your hand!"

—DR. RALPH W. NEIGHBOR, adjunct professor,
Golden Gate Baptist Theological Seminary

This book is dedicated to the memory of Marcus Vegh,

our remarkable colleague, Christian brother, and friend,

who kept showing up at pivotal points in our journey.

December 14, 1959–October 20, 2007

CONTENTS

FOREWORD

To begin with, I was seated cross-legged, a position I have always found uncomfortable since shattering my knee several years ago. I wondered just how long I'd have to remain in that pretzel-like contortion, and if I'd even be able to stand without help when my lecture was completed. The heat in the crowded room was stifling, due in part to the shuttered windows with curtains drawn to keep out both sound and prying eyes. This was the second place we had met in the same number of days as our host was doing everything possible to escape the attention of either neighbors or local authorities.

I looked around the crowded room and into the eyes of loving people who were doing all they could to grasp the meaning of the lesson I was teaching. But I could tell I was not succeeding in driving home my point. *Perhaps it is because I am having to use two interpreters,* I thought to myself, *one to translate the lesson into the national language, and another to translate it from the national language into a local dialect for which there was no alphabet. Or maybe they are just tired,* I continued to muse. *At least I know I am.* I knew these people had not slept in a hotel room as I had, and some of them had just joined the class after traveling for several days.

In reality, I was personally skeptical that this lesson was the one I should be teaching. I had only reluctantly acquiesced to the newly arrived missionary's earnest request. He had heard me teach on this same subject while he was living back in the States. Now he wanted me, his former pastor, to share the same lecture with this group of eager young disciples who made their home up in the mountains. It was there "beyond the clouds" that the people group to whom he'd been assigned dwelled in their longhouses. Excitedly, the new missionary had placed a white board beside me on the floor so I could "draw my chart" and "list my points."

So there I was, struggling through material with which I was intimately acquainted, attempting to teach a lesson I had taught literally hundreds of times before. But I was watching the truth slide out of their agile minds and drop on the floor along with my beads of nervous perspiration. They weren't getting it. I knew it. They knew it. The young missionary knew it . . . and so did his more experienced friend and mentor. That sad day, in spite of great effort and expectations, the truth did not stick. In spite of our greatest hopes, my flat, linear presentation with a brief but clever illustration for each point . . . bombed.

When the facts are on the table, I could have had the same experience related above in virtually any country on the globe and while speaking to those who comprise more than 70 percent of this world's population. Coupled with that fact is the shocking reality that our era of cyber-communication is rapidly creating societies with an educated, high-income, and sophisticated citizenry that communicates "on the fly" and avoids linear reasoning with reckless abandon.

So how do you share what Avery Willis and Mark Snowden graphically portray as "Velcro truth" in our "Teflon world"? For mission-minded evangelicals, the question has ceased being, How we can reach "*those* people"? Now the question is, How can we reach *our world* with the truth, truth that is so in concert with the moving of God's Spirit that it "sticks" and produces supernatural change? As Willis and Snowden explain, the answer to this most important question is, in fact, quite simple. *It is as simple as returning to our Lord's manner of teaching.*

Jesus told *stories*, stories that related to every facet of life, stories that did more than simply illustrate or entertain, stories that could be remembered and repeated. And our Lord's stories contained answers to life's most difficult questions, all the while captivating an audience, riveting its attention to the issue at hand, and providing a mental file for future reference. What's more, the stories Jesus told drew people into a relationship with the Father, requiring simple faith for full understanding. Amazing!

Wouldn't you, like Jesus, want to communicate God's *Velcro truth in this Teflon world?* As you will soon discover, that is not *simply* a privilege to be enjoyed at one's leisure; it is a necessity to be exercised by every believer who sincerely wants to make authentic disciples of our Lord.

Do not turn this page unless you are eager to set out on one of your life's greatest adventures. Everything you have *practiced* will be challenged. But every doctrinal truth you have *believed* will be strengthened. It is with a real sense of urgency and excitement that I challenge you to join the front ranks of those who desire effectiveness in making disciples.

Ready? Then learn how to share *truth that sticks*!

—TOM ELLIFF
Living in the Word
Oklahoma City, Oklahoma

ACKNOWLEDGMENTS

We greatly appreciate so many who have made this book possible.

Shirley, Avery's wife, has been very patient and supportive during this project. Mary Leigh, Mark's wife, invested more than one hundred hours typing up recorded interviews. We are grateful for their love and support.

Val Gresham served as our capable prepublishing editor; she helped us blend our writing styles and added her zeal and insights to the project.

Although we could not tell everyone's story, special appreciation goes to the staff and members of Real Life Ministries in Post Falls, Idaho—especially Jim Putman (senior pastor), Brandon Guindon, Bill Krause, Jim Blazin, Jim Harris, Gene Jacobs, Aaron Couch, Jim Harris, Todd Winslow, Bob Shackelford, and Steve Anderson.

We acknowledge a debt of gratitude to the *Following Jesus: Making Disciples of Oral Learners* team that helped us formulate much of the Bible-storying strategy: Jim Slack, J. O. Terry, Grant Lovejoy, Steve Evans, J. Brandt Smith, Keith Stamps, and Marcus Vegh (www.fjseries .org).

We also want to express our thanks to everyone else who helped us and gave their insights during the manuscript stage: Jim Austin, Richard and Lisa Baker, Linda Bemis, Rick Brekelbaum, Chuck Broughton, Samuel Chiang, Frankie Creel, Steve Douglass, Ralph Ennis, Jonathan Everett, Don Falcos, Bryant Fersner, Ronnie Fox, Gilles Gravelle, Chad and Ashley Hall, Hopp Hopkins, Lynne Abney

Johnson, Caesar Kalinowski, Paul Krueger, Steve Mackey, Charles Madinger, Regina Manley, Iva May, Mike Mohler, Michael Novelli, Lisa Orvis, Jack Popjes, Randy Proctor, Lisa Sells, Ken Sorrells, Dennis Stokes, Wayne Terry, Tracy Turner, and John Walsh.

Our gratitude goes to Bryan Thompson, who graciously consented for us to use the phrase "truth that sticks," which he originally used on his Story4All podcast (www.story4all.com).

A special thank-you goes to the NavPress staff who have brought everything together. We want to express our appreciation to Mike Miller, president, who suggested the need for this book. Our deepest appreciation goes to those who made this book and its distribution better, including Jamie Chavez, Mike Linder, Kris Wallen, and Jessica Chappell. We appreciate your vision and challenge, which led to *Truth That Sticks*.

God was so gracious to hold off Avery's acute leukemia diagnosis until after we finished the book.

BACK TO THE FUTURE

I recently saw a short YouTube clip of a television commercial called "Test Your Awareness."[1] In it, you are asked to count the number of times the basketball team in white passes the ball, while ignoring the actions of the team in black. (The answer is thirteen.) Then, in a thick British accent, the announcer says, "Did you see the moonwalking bear?" When the video is replayed, you see a man dressed in a bear suit moonwalk right through the middle of the teams as they play. I have yet to meet anyone who saw the bear the first time he or she watched the video.

It's an excellent analogy: The moonwalking bear represents the 93 million adults in our midst that we are not aware of—the Americans who don't, won't, or can't read. Half of the adults in the United States can read only the most basic printed material; only one out of three college graduates is a proficient reader.[2] Add to them the millennial generation—those under age twenty-five who are considered literate but prefer oral ways of learning, such as video, movies, music, drama, and social networks—and you understand why this book is a must-read.

Now apply this knowledge to the challenge Christians face. More than half of unchurched Americans tune out approaches from Christian speakers who relate information in the ways *they* prefer to deliver it, rather than in the ways their audience wants to receive it. During the past five years, God has shown us the need to communicate with Americans who prefer oral and visual means. This book offers Christians in America the opportunity and skills to address this need.

We can't ignore the issue any longer. Neither can you. We must communicate the truth of the Bible—the inerrant Word of God—and make it stick. (By *stick*, we mean the ability to remember, recall, interpret, apply, and multiply the Word of God.)

For the past ten years we have worked with more than one hundred missions agencies and thousands of missionaries and missions leaders to address the needs of oral-preference learners in other countries. Along with our colleagues around the world, we have seen an astounding response to oral strategies that effectively communicate the gospel and make disciples in primary oral cultures.[3]

In America, most of the preaching, Bible studies, evangelism, and discipleship is based on linear and sequential thinking conveyed in print media. But our postmodern culture is driving a storytelling revival: We are experiencing a groundswell of social and spiritual change that is largely the result of changes in our learning-style preferences. The majority of the millennials, baby busters/gen Xers, and even many of the baby boomers clearly prefer to learn through spoken and visual means rather than the printed word. Nonetheless, the challenge goes much deeper than just recognizing patterns of preferred communication. The question of the hour is "How do *we* change?" What can we do to help God's truth really stick?

Bible storying is a powerful movement throughout the world, and it's on the rise in mainstream America. We are not theorizing that Bible storying will work. We *know* that it works. This book documents how and why it is *already* working nationwide. Granted, we are still in the early stages, but heavy rains are falling and the water is rising. You can ride the next wave and advance right into the heart of a lost America.

We invite you to come on a journey to discover how to make disciples of oral-preference learners in America. Storying and discipleship each contribute to the process. (By *storying*, we mean the entire process of oral and visual communication, which includes a narrative presentation designed to communicate a Bible story followed by dialogue, interpretation, application, accountability, drama, song, and retelling the story.) The first half of *Truth That Sticks* covers the methods of storying, while the latter half discusses the methods of discipling that make truth stick.

To help make reading this book easier, Avery will tell the story in first person, although the book is coauthored by Mark. Mark has introduced thousands to storying in workshops and has developed an oral Bible—a set of specific Bible stories—for a predominantly Muslim unreached people group. Mark will add further insight in sidebars and include many of the interviews he has done with those utilizing Bible storying in America. Avery and Mark worked together at the International Mission Board, Southern Baptist Convention (SBC), for ten years; served as convener and facilitator, respectively, for the Lausanne workgroup that produced the book *Making Disciples of Oral Learners*; and have worked together through the International Orality Network, of which Avery now serves as executive director.

For the past four years Avery has piloted what we are calling the TruthSticks strategy with Real Life Ministries in Post Falls, Idaho. This remarkable nondenominational church has grown from two couples to more than eight thousand in attendance with seven thousand attending small groups—in just ten years. Because they are the pilot church, we quote people from this church extensively throughout the book. Avery and Mark have also interviewed and studied more than two dozen other churches and ministries in the United States that are using this approach. You will read the stories from leaders and members of

Real Life Ministries throughout the book because we want you to hear from practitioners. You will also be introduced, at the conclusion of the book, to several other books and resources relating to discipling and orality.

There are moments when society changes in significant ways. Successful people capture these moments. They anticipate rather than react. Having the foresight to see a coming wave allows people and organizations to ride it rather than be swept away by it. So what is the future of the Bible-storying approach in the United States? The convergence of storying and discipleship offers a strong clue. May this book provide you with a bridge to those moonwalking among us so you can make disciples of all people.

—AVERY WILLIS AND MARK SNOWDEN

Chapter I

COMMUNICATING VELCRO TRUTH IN A TEFLON WORLD

In the summer of 2000, I was asked a question that changed my life forever. I was at a Billy Graham conference in Amsterdam for evangelists from around the world. The seminar room was buzzing, with six hundred global leaders out of the ten thousand participants hard at work discussing how we could finish the Great Commission in the next ten to fifteen years. We were in the middle of intense discussions when Marcus Vegh, a friend of several years, walked up to me and startled me with that life-changing question. I looked up at his six-foot-three-inch frame and saw his fleeting smile and piercing black eyes as he asked, "Avery, how do you make disciples of oral learners?"

"I don't know," I replied with a shrug of my shoulders. "People have asked me that question for twenty years. I just say, 'I am not working with illiterates. If you are, figure it out.'"

"It's been twenty years, and no one has done it," Marcus retorted. "You know about discipleship. Avery, it's your job. Seventy percent of the unreached people in the world are oral learners."

I heard his voice as if it were the voice of God. I am not sure why this question hit me so hard. As senior vice president for overseas operations with the International Mission Board of Southern Baptists (IMB), I was leading more than five thousand missionaries to focus on reaching the unreached. I was aware of oral learners but had never considered them to be my responsibility. Now I heard God telling me otherwise.

Little did I realize that addressing the challenge of discipling oral learners cross-culturally would solve a close-to-home problem I had wrestled with for more than forty years: how to make disciples in America—and not just with people who can't or won't read, but also with millennials under twenty-five who don't like to read books.

As this book unfolds, I invite you to discover with me how the fundamentals of first-century discipleship affect our efforts to make disciples as Jesus did—in the twenty-first century. Get ready for some eye-popping discoveries!

MAKING TRUTH STICK

God made truth to stick more tightly than Velcro. Unfortunately, we live in a Teflon world.

Velcro was invented by George de Mestral in Switzerland. During a vacation in 1944, he took his dog for a walk. When he returned, he had to pull cockleburs from the dog's fur and his own clothing. He wondered why the burrs were so hard to separate from the clothing and fur. De Mestral took one of the burrs and put it under a microscope. He noticed that tiny hooks covered the burr's surface; when these hooks hit the loops of his sock's fabric, they stuck tightly. It took him ten years to figure out how to manufacture the system of tiny nylon hooks and loops that he called Velcro. If you look at a piece of Velcro, you will see that one side has loops and the other has hooks. This fastening system is now used in multitudes of ways, from securing meal trays on NASA spacecraft to holding car dashboards in place.[1]

At the other extreme, Teflon was accidentally created by a scientist trying to produce a more effective coolant gas. He discovered a material that was extremely slippery and resistant to corrosive chemicals. This slippery quality is what makes Teflon unique. Insects cannot even walk up the side of a wall that is coated with it. When a housewife saw her chemist husband treating his fishing tackle with Teflon to minimize tangling, she asked him to spray some on her frying pan. The rest is history. Food and cooking oils don't stick to a surface covered with Teflon coating.[2]

So what do Velcro and Teflon have to do with truth? God wired our brains with "loops" so that His truth could fasten to our lives. He put "hooks" in the way the Bible is communicated—both by the authors' inspired messages and the processes He has shown us—so that truth will stick. God intended for us to use our sensory learning loops—sight, hearing, touch, smell, and taste—to remember His Word. Through our senses we learn, remember, and repeat things to others. The first part of this book will show how Bible-storying loops (see storying in the glossary on page 207) can maximize the use of our senses and other abilities God gave us to remember His Word. The second part of the book will explore the discipleship hooks God gave us to obey and apply His truth.

The problem is that we live in a Teflon world in which information glides off our brains like water off a freshly waxed BMW. The deluge of information we are faced with today puts a coating over the normal loops that would help us retain God's truths. This exponential growth of information causes teachers to teach, "You don't have to remember all this information; just know where to find it." In our Teflon world our hooks and loops have become as slick as polished hardwood floors as we slippy-slide in our stockinged feet through endless expanses of information.

Marketers often talk about "punching through the clutter." What they mean is getting their message to catapult past the messages put there by other communicators. Our senses are bombarded from daybreak until midnight. Or in the case of social media like Twitter, a new experience this minute simply becomes the next line on the text screen of life. The "Teflonization" of America—including the people of God—keeps the information sliding away.

Hear a derogatory remark? Just let it slide. Fight with your wife? Spend an hour in therapy. Hurt your knee at soccer practice? Do as Peyton Manning says: "Just rub some dirt on it. You'll be okay." Hear a sermon? Enjoy the emotional tug, but wonder what's for lunch or whether the pastor will finish in time for the start of the NFL game. Go to a Bible study? No problem—just scan through the booklet, get the gist, and crack enough jokes to make the hour pass quickly. And you're the teacher! Time for refreshments yet?

When you realize how fast the quantity of information is growing, you understand the difficulty Christian leaders have trying to get people to remember God's Word. There are about 540,000 words in the English language. That is about five times as many as during Shakespeare's day. It is estimated that a week's worth of *The New York Times* contains more information than a person in the eighteenth century was likely to come across in a lifetime. The amount of technical information is doubling every two years. For students starting a four-year technical degree, this means half of what they learn as freshmen will be outdated by their third year of study![3]

The accelerating growth of digital information is overwhelming. Research shows that the first commercial text message was sent in December 1992, but today the number of daily text messages exceeds the population of the planet. It took thirty-eight years for radio to reach an audience of 50 million, television only thirteen years, and the computer four years. But Apple's iPod took only three years to reach 50 million people; Facebook did it in two. In 2006, 2.7 billion searches a month were performed on Google.[4]

Don't throw up your hands and quit reading. There is hope . . . but not yet!

THE TEFLON WORLD OF THE CHURCH

Today, American society appears to be literate, but very few things stick in our minds. Our learning loops in the Velcro analogy have become so coated over we cannot easily remember what we are taught. For example, do you remember the main points of the pastor's sermon last Sunday? And if you are the pastor, do you remember your points from three weeks ago? The sermons aren't sticking to the remaining loops that still exist in our Teflon-coated minds.

In a workshop on storying the Bible, I copied six random pages out of a novel and gave them to six participants to read aloud. When they finished, I asked the group to retell the story of the novel. They told me some facts and parts of the story, but they could not tell me the novel's plot. I said, "You just saw demonstrated how much Bible knowledge the majority of church members have. They know about some stories, such as Samson, David and Goliath, Noah and the flood, and Jesus feeding the five thousand, but they don't have a clue about how all the stories fit together to make one story of the Bible panorama."

In America today, 60 percent of the general population could not list five of the Ten Commandments, and half of all high school seniors thought Sodom and Gomorrah were married.[5]

And Christians are not much better. They not only fail to know the information but have slipped in their beliefs regarding it. Because Americans are increasingly weak in their Bible knowledge, they are creating their own theology. In August 2008, the Barna Group learned that four out of ten people who professed to be Christians said that Satan does not exist but merely represents evil; this same group indicated that they agreed with a statement that Jesus sinned during His earthly ministry. When it came to the Holy Spirit, more than half (58 percent) said that the Holy Spirit was not real. One-third of all Christians in America, who indicate that they believe the Bible is totally accurate in its principles, say that the Qur'an and the Book of Mormon are based on the same spiritual truths.[6] Millions who claim to be Christians believe repentance for sins and belief in Christ are essential for salvation, but they also believe that a person could do enough good works to merit salvation.[7]

Hidden in Plain View

On a plane from Detroit to Atlanta, I sat next to Brandon. He holds a degree in biomechanics from Vanderbilt University and was working on a master's at Georgia Tech. He described himself as a Christian and, yes, he owned a Bible, although he never read it. Brandon admitted that he had only been exposed to the Bible in homilies at mass. When he brought up the differences between salvation by works or faith, I had a choice: lecture on doctrine or story God's truth.

I asked him if he had ever heard Jesus' parable of the prodigal son in Luke 15:11-32. He had never heard the story but encouraged me to tell it to him. He smiled as I quietly talked him through the story of the wayward son, his forgiving father, and the jealous older brother. Rather than argue doctrine, I conveyed God's truth in a Bible story. Brandon caught the meaning right away. Here was a bright twenty-four-year-old who was transfixed by a story and moved by its implications of faith. And, sadly, the story had previously existed only in the unknown realm of a Bible on his bookshelf.

—Mark

READING ON THE DECLINE

People are increasingly choosing to receive information in nonprint forms. Even though the majority of Americans can read, many of them cannot read with adequate comprehension. The U.S. Department of Education researched 18,500 people in 2003 and determined that less than half of all Americans can handle "continuous prose"[8]—and it has been estimated that the Bible is 75 percent continuous prose. (See appendix for startling information regarding literacy in the United States.)

In 2004 the National Endowment for the Arts (NEA) held a press conference at the New York Public Library. NEA chairperson Dana Gioia stated the obvious: "America can no longer take active and engaged literacy for granted."[9] She then reported on a reading-related research project of seventeen thousand adults in the United States. Only one in three American men is reading literature of any kind, and women are not reading like they used to either. In fact, over the past twenty years, 20 million people have completely stopped reading. That means that, at this rate, we are losing the capacity to communicate with a million people a year using literate means. The largest drop in reading rates was among young adults, age eighteen to twenty-four, compared to the rest of the adult population. Overall, less than *half* of all Americans read literature such as the Bible.[10] Only an elite 14 percent still read extensively—and two-thirds of college graduates fail to read with proficiency. A 2004 study reports that "literary reading in America is not only declining rapidly among all groups, but the rate of decline has accelerated, especially among the young."[11] This reflects a significant shift toward nonprint media for entertainment, information gathering, and education.

People scan written material for items of interest, evaluate them quickly, and then look for a summary or hyperlink to a related topic. How do you think such skimming over the Scriptures affects spiritual development? In contrast, I am astounded by how many young people discuss the plots of hundreds of movies and pepper their everyday speech with lines from famous actors. The greatest influence on our worldview today is clearly the entertainment industry. Why is it that TV reality shows dominate water-cooler discussions? The explosion of ever-present music and podcasts through MP3 players such as iPods is a marketing phenomenon. Marketing strategists target our God-given loops with their versions of truth. Sadly, instead of using those loops to disciple people, the church virtually ignores using them to disciple adults.

Those of us whose jobs require reading in the marketplace seldom, if ever, pick up a book—including the Bible—for pleasure reading when we get home. Eighty percent of American families did not buy a book last year, and the average reader only makes it to page 18.[12] The incredible power of online search engines accelerates our ability to find what we need, but in reality we don't take the time to invest in serious reading.

It's as if we have become characters from the movie *The Matrix*. We expect that if we need to know how to do something, we'll just plug in and download whatever we need, whenever it is needed. Need to operate a helicopter? No problem, just download this program directly to the brain and, voilà, like the heroine Trinity, we'll be off and flying effortlessly.

That's depressing news for those of us who take seriously Jesus' Great Commission to make disciples of all peoples. When I heard that electrifying question, I discovered I had just explored the slick surface of the problem—making truth stick in a Telfon world. It felt like I was trying to put together a puzzle, but a lot of the pieces were missing.

QUESTIONS FOR REFLECTION

1. Do you have a Velcro mind or a Teflon mind in regard to biblical truth? What makes you say that?
2. How can we make truth stick in the twenty-first century?
3. In your experience, what percentage of each of the following categories would you characterize as biblically illiterate: teenagers, students, adults, and seniors?
4. How do you make disciples in the twenty-first century?

CHAPTER 2

WIRED FOR STORIES

After Marcus asked me how to make disciples of oral learners, I kept rolling the question around in my mind all during lunch and then later in my room. I knew that the problem was not just retaining information. Communicating information to people who remember it does not make them disciples. But people do have to retain information before they can apply it, don't they?

I had a flashback to a visit I made to Oklahoma City eight years earlier to see Tom Elliff. We were close friends and wanted to talk about what God was doing in our lives. Tom opened the door as wide as the grin on his face. He grabbed my arm and pulled me inside.

"You have got to see this!" he shouted excitedly. "It's great!"

"What? What are you talking about?" I said as I caught my breath.

"This video I've been watching. It's *EE-Taow*!"

"E-what?" I asked as I settled into my comfortable seat on his couch.

For the next hour I sat captivated by the story of the gospel coming to an unreached people group in Papua New Guinea. New Tribes missionaries Mark and Gloria Zook entered the world of the Mouk people in 1983. The video begins with the account of how the Zooks learned the Mouk worldview. A man dressed up in a large mask is dancing with other men in the village. These men told the Mouk women that the dancer with the mask was the spirit of a dead ancestor who had returned. If a woman implied at any time that the masked dancer was not the spirit of an ancestor, or if she ever saw the mask by itself, the punishment was death by strangulation, carried out by her male relatives. Lies and deception were core values of the male-dominated culture.

After months of intense culture and language study, Mark and Gloria were ready to communicate God's Word with the Mouk people, but they asked themselves the question, "How?" The Bible is an intricate book, they reasoned, and none of the Mouk people had any previous exposure to it. They decided to just tell the stories of the Bible in chronological order to the entire village of 310 people who gathered each morning and evening. Over the next weeks the Mouk people developed a sincere reverence for God and feared daily that God might rightly destroy them because of their sins. For the first two months Mark shared Old Testament stories in chronological order before he finally introduced Jesus Christ as the Savior, born as a baby in Bethlehem. "As we told the stories of the life of Christ, they fell in love with Him, and Jesus became the Mouk's hero," Mark said. "They loved Him, and they idolized Him."

At times the Mouk people were so intent on the stories and their meaning that they stopped eating and would not even sleep. They spent every waking moment discussing the message and listening over and over again to the lessons that had been recorded daily on cassette tape.

The Mouk people were upset when they heard the story of Judas and how he betrayed Jesus, leading to His trial before Pilate. They had faith, though, that Jesus would somehow escape. Mark said, "Tomorrow we will finish our talk."

Early the next morning, Mark told the villagers the story of Jesus' crucifixion and the resurrection. With no break, he then went back through the Old Testament stories, starting with Abel and his sacrifice that was accepted by God. When he got to the story of Abraham and Isaac, Mark shared that just as a real lamb was substituted for Isaac, Jesus' death and blood was shed as the Mouks' substitution. At that point, the lights really went on. Mark could see and hear the people responding. "*EE-Taow! EE-Taow!* ["It's true (or good); it's very true!"],"* they shouted. Mark stood in their midst and asked them what they thought. From all over the crowd came their responses: "I believe! I believe!"

That day almost the entire village believed in Jesus and accepted Him as Savior and Lord. Contrary to the normally restrained nature of the Mouk people, spontaneous celebration and rejoicing broke out. "*EE-Taow!*" they shouted over and over again as they jumped up and down en masse. "*EE-Taow! EE-Taow!*" This celebration lasted for two and a half hours.

A second video showed the rest of the story. Mark spoke up as the celebrating crowd jostled him. He asked some of the men, "When are you going to go and tell the other villages about the good news?" Everyone got quiet.

Finally one man stepped up and said, "Yes, we will go, but we don't know how to go about it."

Mark replied, "That's all I wanted to know. I will show you how."

Spontaneous celebration broke out again.

After a few days of training, the men who were learning to teach assisted Mark as he shared the stories in the next village. In the third village the men told the stories, and Mark assisted. The Word of God continued to spread to twelve surrounding tribes, many of them with different languages.[1]

"That's it!" I shouted. "That's what we need all over the world!" I compared this account to the way we preach the same message in our churches to stoic crowds who don't get it. The contrast was obvious.

In Amsterdam, I reflected on that experience eight years earlier, and I realized the video of that amazing movement of God had become only a precious memory and a sermon illustration for me. It had had no personal application for me. I repented and vowed to help Christians tell the stories of Jesus to the nations.

When I returned to the United States to my job of leading the overseas operations of the IMB, I called together eight missionary storying practitioners from around the world who had refined Mark Zook's approach with great effectiveness. Over the next three years this group (which included coauthor Mark Snowden) developed an oral approach to discipling using Bible stories and recorded more than four hundred audio Bible stories. We called our set of stories *Following Jesus: Making Disciples of Oral Learners*[2] and showed people how to adapt it for any culture.

WHAT ABOUT AMERICA?

However, I had not been able to connect the experience of the Mouk people in Papua New Guinea with the reality of American church life. As we saw unparalleled success overseas during the next several years, I began to wonder, *If Mark Zook could disciple a primary oral tribal society in the jungles of Papua New Guinea with Bible stories, could God use the same methods to communicate with modern audiences? Is storying just a third-world methodology? Or would it work equally well with people who are literate to varying degrees?* This concept was worth exploring. I felt like I was putting together a puzzle, and I had just found a key piece to making disciples anywhere: storying!

IMMERSED IN STORIES

The first piece of my puzzle was the realization that God wired us for stories. Everyone loves a story—even adults. When someone says, "Let me tell you a story . . ." everyone's ears perk up. When a speaker talks in abstract terms, our minds demand an example. When I told a longtime friend about what I was learning about storying, he related to me the Bible story of Naaman that I had told in his church thirty years earlier. Most of my messages aren't remembered thirty minutes or thirty days later, let alone thirty years.

What is it about stories that helps us remember them? We all have a story, complete with interesting characters and lots of plot twists. Stories reflect not only our own reality but also other people's. They help us interpret life, learn vicariously through the truths we can draw from the story, and change—sometimes for the better, sometimes for the worse if they're the wrong stories. Bible stories provide Christians a way to view life so that we can learn from very real people who dealt with situations just like we face. Stephen Stringer, a veteran storyteller, said, "A picture is worth a thousand words; a story is worth a thousand pictures."[3] Recognizing that God has wired us to understand reality best through stories becomes the first step in making God's truth stick.

Bible Storying with Students

After ten years in youth ministry, I felt as though I'd tried everything to help my students connect with the Bible. When a missionary named John Witte taught me the art of Chronological Bible Storying, I realized it was more than just a new way to teach. It was a complete shift in how I could help students with their spiritual formation.

It changed everything about the way I now look at my faith and ministry. I have led youth and adults in this process, and almost all were captivated by it. Guided by imaginative listening, creative retellings, and interactive discussions, storying inspired my groups (and me) to find themselves in God's Story. Without question, it continues to be the most transformative method of learning I have seen in twenty years of ministry, and now I have been able to help 1,500 other youth ministries use it.[4]

—Michael Novelli, author of *Shaped by the Story*

MEMORY HOOKS: A STORY TO REMEMBER

A college friend showed me how a story can give you a framework to remember a list of things. I tried it with a large audience. I told them, "Choose any ten things and tell them to me only one time. Then I will recite the items back to you, forward or backward." As the audience called out the items, someone wrote them on a whiteboard behind me. Then I asked how they wanted me to repeat them. At their request I gave them in order and then gave the even-numbered objects forward and the odd-numbered objects backward. The audience gasped and clapped when I recited every answer perfectly. Then I told them, "I have a very ordinary memory, and sometimes my wife even questions that!" When they asked me how I did it, I said, "A friend in college showed me how to remember lists, but he told me I was never to tell anyone how I did it." They groaned and protested. I smiled and said, "Since I have forgotten his name, I'll tell you."

It's really very simple. My friend told me to make up a story in which I mentally go to several places in my daily routine and number each place in sequence. My story started in my dorm room when I woke up and stretched out across the campus throughout my day. The numbers on the locations never changed. When I heard the first item,

I pictured it in my clothes closet, which is the first station in my story. When you mentioned the second one, I imagined that object in my bed. The third station was where I looked out my second-floor window. The fourth station was the restroom, and so on. As you can imagine, some of these imaginary pictures are ludicrous. The more absurd, the easier they are to remember. To recall ten or twenty items, I just mentally play the movie of my day's story in my mind and find the items that I have placed in the numbered stations all along the way. Anyone can do it. You can make up your own story and remember your numbered stations.

As our *Following Jesus* group of Bible storyers began to wrestle with the truth that stories should be used in discipleship because they are easily remembered, I realized why my story game had worked. Remembering a story is easy because it involves a spatial sequence. It engages your imagination. It's fun. It gives me a visual framework to "hang" things on as I just walk through my daily routine. I realized that Bible stories do the same thing for God's truth. After we tell a Bible story to a group and ask them questions about it, they are able to hang truth on the locations, events, people, or dialogue in the story. The story and the dialogue help God's truth stick.

ORAL TRADITION AND THE BIBLE

Have you ever wondered why more than half the Bible is narrative? God had it written that way so that the 90-plus percent of the people in biblical times who were nonreaders could remember it.

God has been transmitting His truths for centuries. Yet I can find only three times in the Bible when God or Jesus wrote anything: the Ten Commandments, the handwriting on the wall in Daniel, and when Jesus wrote in the sand in front of the woman caught in adultery—and what He wrote there was not even recorded. On the other hand, the phrase "thus saith the Lord" is repeated 414 times in the

King James Version.[5] God speaks to everyone orally, and He gave us the Old Testament as a written record of what existed for centuries, most of it first in a purely oral form. In fact, the Jewish scribes trusted their memories more than any writing surface that could be eaten by bugs, consumed by fire, or flawed by a false stroke. It was not good enough for a scribe just to be able to copy correctly; he had to quote the text verbatim.

The Gospels of the New Testament were conveyed by word of mouth for decades before they were put into written form. Matthew, Mark, Luke, and John all wrote the story of Jesus from their perspectives. These authors lived within a culture that constantly told these stories whenever believers met. Parents told them to their children. Friends told them to friends. Mature believers told them to people who were new to the faith. There was a "group memory" that self-corrected any deviation from the facts of the stories. When God had them written down though holy men inspired by the Holy Spirit, He permanently recorded them for all time so we can be sure that they are correct today.

It occurred to me in my discovery process that we say we want to make disciples as Jesus did. But how do we reconcile our approach with Jesus' approach? "Jesus spoke all these things to the crowd in parables; he did not say anything to them without using a parable" (Matthew 13:34). To help Nicodemus understand the role of faith in salvation, Jesus told him the story of Moses lifting up a snake on a pole to cure a plague. When questioned about divorce, Jesus returned to the story of Adam and Eve to point out that wedded couples become one flesh. Jesus told the disciples about how He rebuffed Satan with Scripture that specifically addressed each temptation, and He told them about His struggle in the Garden of Gethsemane; otherwise they would never have known.

In their book *Made to Stick* Chip and Dan Heath make a lengthy case for why we remember some ideas many years after we initially hear about them. Chip is a professor at Stanford University, and his brother Dan is a former researcher at Harvard Business School and is a consultant at Duke Corporate Education. They use a clever acronym—SUCCESs—that fits into our puzzle for making God's truth stick. Truth that sticks displays the following qualities:

S—Simple
U—Unexpected
C—Concrete
C—Credible
E—Emotional
S—Stories
s

Yes, they said stories. Stories are a key component to making ideas stick. Chip and Dan point out that hearing stories serves as a kind of mental flight simulator, preparing us to respond more quickly and effectively.[6] Stories make things stick.

We now know the importance of stories to facilitate learning. But how can we go from centuries of focusing on literate ways of communication in our churches back to making truth stick with stories in modern times?

Come discover the secrets of making truth stick in the lives of everyone.

QUESTIONS FOR REFLECTION

1. Why are stories so powerful in your life?
2. Think of the different ways Jesus used stories. How could you use stories as Jesus did to improve your communication and the memory of what you said?
3. Which parts of the SUCCESs acronym do you currently use to make God's truth stick?

CHAPTER 3

USING THE SENSORY GATES

I knew intuitively that stories were an important piece of the puzzle of making truth stick, but how could I square that with my literate approach to ministry? I had invested twenty-six years in school to get the highest degrees the educational system offered. I had spent more than forty years speaking, writing, and teaching—all with a literate bias. Good grief, I had been president of a seminary and the adult discipleship director for a denominational publishing house; I had written eighteen books and was in the process of writing another. I used the skill of literacy almost every waking moment. Was that wrong?

No, literacy is not wrong for the 33 percent of the world's people who prefer to receive their information in a written form. It fits. But it began to sink in that using only literate methods had limited me from communicating to the other four billion people—*two-thirds of the world*—who can't, don't, or won't read! By depending on literate methodologies, my missionary colleagues and I had limited our ministries primarily to literates or semiliterates. Worse than that, we compounded the problem overseas by teaching literate people who were members of primary oral cultures to make disciples using literate means, thereby limiting their effectiveness in their own oral societies.

BRINGING IT HOME

An equally disturbing discovery was that my dependence on literacy had limited me to a single mode of communication that did not work well with the majority of Americans who don't read complex books, such as the Bible. That dependency also restricted me from communicating to the rising digital generation that prefers visual/oral communication over more literate means. Literacy is a way of thinking that literate persons use to express themselves. Proficient literates use analytical statements, expositional details, and logical lists—not just what is written down.

This challenged my assumptions about learning. I had been taught that literate means are superior and oral means are inferior. How could I go back to what I perceived to be the simplistic communication process that oral-preference learners used? Or was I looking at this problem from the wrong side? Bible stories are used in literate communication, too, although in the religious world these stories are usually one-dimensional and flat. Literacy has some distinct advantages, but I wondered, *Are some oral methods more effective in communicating truth?*

USE ALL THE SENSES

God designed us to use all of our senses to make His truth stick. Velcro works because it uses multiple hooks and loops. Although using all of our senses for learning should be self-evident, we often substitute literate explanations for the use of sensory learning. When we use only literate forms, we make tenuous connections between facts; these are easily forgotten. For example, the primary ways of communicating truth in preaching are:

- One-way communication, with the hearers unable to respond
- Word analysis
- Expositional arguments
- Bible stories as illustrations more than content
- Use of outlines — three points and a poem
- Lists — like this!

What if we used stories the way Jesus did? What if we used all of our senses to make truth stick? Velcro won't stay together well unless the two sides are pressed firmly together. However, if a two-inch square of Velcro *is* pressed firmly together, it can hold a 175-pound man on a wall!

In our churches, we tend to focus our communication upon a single touch point — literate statements, even though they are communicated orally. However, people can more easily embrace God's ways when they can see, hear, smell, taste, and touch the gospel. We need to press God's biblical truth hooks into our sensory loops, through personal interaction and vicarious experiences.

Through a Child's Eyes

When our daughter was young, we belonged to a new church that met in a school. All week long, my wife and I taught her Bible stories, showed her Christian videos, sang Bible songs, and prayed with her using words she could understand. At Sunday school her teachers were well prepared with activities and interacted with her personally.

The Bible was presented in story form, using pictures and other visual aids. The children often did artwork that depicted some aspect of the story. They sang songs that reinforced its theme. Our daughter followed the narrative with interest and could easily repeat the story on the way home. She caught it.

When we took our daughter into the worship service, however, the experience was no longer geared to her learning preferences. The preacher gave his sermon from behind a podium while she was expected to be quiet and patiently listen. Our pastor usually spoke on a theme, pulling from different Bible verses. Her mother and I thought he was a good preacher, but my daughter never talked about one sermon. We had to give her pictures to color to keep her quiet. And the catch is, there were very few sermons that my wife and I actually discussed in detail because they were so highly expositional.

— Mark

Compare Mark and Mary Leigh's daughter's experiences in Sunday school with the worship service and ask yourself, "What is wrong with this picture?" You might say, "But she was just a child and could not understand the deep truths the pastor was teaching." I would agree, to some extent, that is true, but let me ask you — which do you listen to more attentively and enjoy more: the children's story the pastor tells or the regular sermon? Jesus communicated the most profound truths through stories. I have discovered that people with PhDs also love to hear carefully told Bible stories and that you can then go as deep in meaning as you like in the dialogue if you ask the right questions. Why do we shift our learning methodologies to a literate-only approach when children are about eleven or twelve years old? With the explosion of electronic communication, those under twenty-five aren't relating to it anymore.

Some object, saying, "But you are just telling stories; you have to teach them the Word of God." Excuse me! The Bible stories *are* the Word of God. God has chosen to implant His truth in our lives and on our lips through stories. Can you imagine a Bible without the stories? In the Old Testament all you would have left is the Law, Psalms, some Wisdom Literature, and some pronouncements of the prophets. In the New Testament you would have the teachings of Jesus and a few sermons in Acts and most of the Epistles, but no stories that put them in context. Remember, history is narrative.

If there were no stories, what would the nature of our Bible be? It could be seen as a rule book with propositional truth and thus become a legalistic directive. Or it could be used like the Koran, which Islam says should be memorized whether or not you understand it.

But God put His truth in story form as well as propositional truth. I am so glad God communicated to us the way He made us—to love stories and especially His story.

STORYING TO AN AUDIENCE

We are familiar with the response—or lack of response—to a typical literate church service. Let's compare that with what I did with an audience of several hundred people spanning all generations and forty races at the Youth With A Mission (YWAM) base in Kona, Hawaii. I set up the story of Jonah by telling of my personal experience of going to within fifteen miles of the historical site of Nineveh in Iraq. While there, I realized what it meant for Jonah to go to Nineveh. I reflected on all the reasons he didn't want to go. Nineveh was hundreds of miles across the desert—a long way from Jonah's home. It was hot and uncomfortable there. The Ninevites were terrorists and Israel's hated enemies. Jonah did not want God to forgive them. Because he knew that God was a compassionate and forgiving God, he was afraid that God might do just that. Jonah wanted no part of it! Sharing the setting from my experience made Jonah come alive for them.

Because my audience was focused on reaching the world with the gospel, I showed a short video of the 840 unreached people groups in the Middle East and North Africa. The video closed with the question "Will you be the one to take the gospel to these unreached people groups and multiply disciples among Muslims?" I had the group's attention, and they were ready for the story.

I said, "Close your Bibles and listen to the story of Jonah carefully, because I will select five people from the audience at the end of the story to come up on stage and answer questions about it. I won't know who you are until I finish, so you better listen." I also alerted the music director and band that I would like for them to listen and create a song about the story by the time we finished.

I told the story of Jonah as accurately as I could in my own words, including the biblical dialogue of the characters. I moved around on the stage to represent the places Jonah went. Then I invited five representatives of different ages and races up to the stage. First I asked them questions about the facts in the story until they remembered them in sequence. The members of the audience were busy checking their Bibles to see if I had told the story correctly! The audience loved seeing the representatives put on the spot and laughed with them at their answers. Then I asked the five people a number of interpretation questions, such as "Why didn't Jonah want to obey God and go to Nineveh?" and "Who is the hero of this story?" I moved on to application questions like "Why don't we want to go to the unreached people groups in the Middle East?" They said our reasons for not going were the same as Jonah's. I asked, "What should we do differently because of this story?" They all came to the conclusion that we should obey God the first time, regardless of what He tells us to do.

After the questions, I called on volunteers to act out the story spontaneously as best they could while the rest of the audience played the part of the Ninevites. As the volunteers were coming to the platform, I asked the musicians if they were ready to sing the song they had created.

The director exclaimed, "Now?"

"Yes."

"Make up a song on the spot, in front of three hundred people?"

"Yes, you can do it," I said. "Get together with the band while we enact the story and be ready with a song by the time we are finished!"

The reenactment was a blast! Each person added his or her own personality to the story. A ten-year-old girl from the Virgin Islands volunteered to do the voice of God. She made her voice as deep as she could and solemnly declared God's pronouncements. Everyone loved it. You can imagine how the interactions turned out between those playing the roles of the whale and Jonah, the people of Nineveh and Jonah, and the vine and Jonah. When we finished the story, I asked what the actors had left out and what they had added, just to be sure everyone knew what was actually in the Bible story instead of how the people had answered questions or spoken during the drama. I did that to be sure they remembered the story correctly.

When the band and musicians came up with a blues number about Jonah—"I won't go, no, no, no!"—the entire place was rocking!

To close the service, I showed a video clip of the testimony of a survivor of a Muslim terrorist attack in which four of our IMB missionaries were killed outside Mosul, the modern Nineveh. In the video, Carrie McDonald, who lost her husband and was still recovering from her wounds, said with emotion, "My Jesus wears scars on His body from the violence He endured. How can we sit back and say, 'I can't,' because it's too hard? Especially when the world is saying, 'You just can't do that.'" She paused, gathered her strength, and said with fortitude, "Trust me, for my Jesus, it is the least that I can do."[1]

Scores of people responded that night to the call to go as missionaries to the hard places of the world. As the session closed, I invited people to come to the front and get a sprig of a vine similar to the one that God grew over Jonah so they could remember and meditate on the message of the story. I tried to use as many sensory experiences as possible.

To this day, people come up to me in various places around the world and talk about that experience. I think you could have the greatest preacher in the world preach on Jonah and not affect lives the way that experience did. Why? Because God designed us to use all of our senses to make truth stick. Although the use of the senses should be self-evident, our practice often substitutes literate explanations for the use of sensory learning. Even when we literates use stories, we usually don't tell them well. We summarize them. We leave out all the juicy sensory details. They are right there in the Bible because it was written primarily to people immersed in an oral world. We just ignore them.

To quote Samuel Chiang of the International Orality Network, "Our God of details left this record for us in this way; we have reduced it, sound-bite sized it, and summarized it so much to our detriment that we no longer have a high regard for God's Word."[2] In other words, we rush past those details of sight, sound, hearing, and touch to get to the meaning of the story.

Don't get me wrong. I am not proposing that every sermon could or should be like the example above. The process I described works best in a small-group setting. I am not putting down expository preaching, but I *am* asking, "How can we use all the senses in all our presentations to make truth stick?" Let's look briefly at the sensory gates. In succeeding chapters of this book we will show you how to use all of the sensory gates in a small-group setting to make disciples as Jesus did.

Hearing

Hearing is one of our most important sensory gates. When we actively listen, we imagine the story as it is being told. Oral-preference learners imagine themselves being *inside* the story. When we hear a theme and sing a song about it, the meaning goes deeper into our subconscious minds. I am often surprised when I find myself humming or singing a song and realize that it fits my current situation exactly. Then I recognize that a phrase my mind has picked up is buried down in the song. Somehow the Holy Spirit has used my subconscious mind to recall a song that matches just what I needed for the situation. Ethnomusicologists (people who study cultural differences in music) point out that beat, rhythm, use of instruments, clapping, humming, whistling, and even interpretive movements (dance) are all part of experiencing not only the music but also the message the music conveys.

Sight

Sight is an additional on-ramp for learning. When a story is told dramatically and with emotion, we imagine it—and it is hard to forget. Pictures in a book or on a screen can add further visual detail to the story. If we see a drama of the story, it helps us picture the event and the action. If we are actually one of the characters in a spontaneous enactment of the story, we see it even more clearly and feel it more deeply.

Touch

Touch is a good way to make abstract ideas more concrete. If you can let the hearers touch selected items, their minds associate the story with things from the real world; this helps a truth or a story stick. Handling physical items as diverse as a whip, thorns, a hammer, or nails related to the Crucifixion, for example, help the participants visualize the story. Touch is a memory container, especially when you extend touch to include the emotions, such as when we say we were touched by the story.

Smell and Taste

The senses of smell and taste are not as easily incorporated into learning experiences, but it is possible, especially if we help people use their imaginations. We can call on people to imagine the smell of fresh bread and the distinct odor of fish when Jesus fed the five thousand, or the smell of the stable where Jesus was born. The senses of taste and smell can also be utilized in the Lord's Supper or at a "Taste of Missions" festival when people sample ethnic foods from around the world. Such experiences can open up a discussion on missions in a very inviting way.

USING THE SENSORY GATES: A CASE STUDY

As a professional storyteller, John Walsh added to Bible stories whatever he felt would make them better. Then he attended a Bible-storying seminar; now he is committed to telling the Bible stories accurately without embellishing them.

John experimented with two churches to see if a congregation could be structured so the people would interact with Bible stories at a high level. He enlisted his own church, Calvary Baptist Church in Normal, Illinois, with an average attendance of nine hundred people. Calvary Baptist used thirty-six stories of the life of Christ—four semesters of nine stories each. The second church was Hope Alliance Church in Bloomington, Illinois, with about thirty members. Hope Alliance started with thirty-six Old Testament stories the first year, continued with thirty-six life-of-Christ stories the second year, and then used thirty-six stories from the book of Acts and the Epistles the third year.

Calvary developed twenty teams—drama, music, Bible storying, research, poetry, art, and so forth. These teams were to interact with each story and minister to the congregation accordingly. For every story, the writing team created five devotionals to be read the week before the story was used in church. The devotional book suggested activities to do at home to help people internalize each story. The following Sunday was given totally to that one Bible story. All classes taught the story, and the pastor preached on it. The drama team developed short plays to be incorporated into the church service. The research team put interesting facts in the bulletin, along with a weekly poem from the poetry team. A detailed version of research notes went on the website. And so it went with all twenty teams.

To summarize their efforts, John said,

The idea was for a larger number of people to get involved in what was being taught in the church. It worked! People interacted with the story according to their individual interests. The pastoral staff didn't have to beg people to get involved. The people did it! They rose to leadership in an unbelievable way. The pastors could focus on their responsibility—preaching the story! When a family drove away from the church, all members of the family had spent significant time in the same Bible story.

Each child was given a card with a simple version of the story and tips on how to tell it. It had a place for others to sign if the child told them the story. Kids loved it. Some went into the public schools and told stories. One girl went into her mother's beauty shop where she had a natural audience.

The following week, teenage volunteers gathered the cards. They stamped the children's "passports" if they had told the story. The kids even had races to see how many times they could tell it from Sunday to Sunday. Even the teenage volunteers, who were asked only to be monitors, told the stories and got their cards signed.[3]

At Hope Alliance, the storytellers told the story during the church service, and the pastor preached on it. They did an excellent job retelling the story with music. The congregation met in small groups the following week and discussed the story, which helped the members grow. As a smaller church, they didn't have the resources Calvary had, but John said the impact was deeper, since they went through the whole Bible the first year, and the life of Christ, and the book of Acts and the Epistles in the succeeding years.

The pastor of Hope Alliance told John, "I am totally sold on this way of 'doing church.' We will never go back to how we did things before."[4]

Now I had found another piece of the puzzle for making God's truth stick—getting beyond the one-dimensional methods of literate communication in order to use the sensory gates to help make truth stick like Velcro. In the next chapter we will talk about another piece of the puzzle—using small groups to bring the Bible to life and getting the story inside people.

QUESTIONS FOR REFLECTION

1. How could you use stories and the senses to help people bring the Bible to life?
2. Read the account of the story of Jonah I told and discern how each action helped the truth to stick.
3. Look at the brief description of the five senses and write in the margin a percentage of how much of your last presentation used that sense.

CHAPTER 4

MAKING THE BIBLE COME TO LIFE

How do you bring the Bible to life? This question has always intrigued me. Now I also began to wonder, *With all the twenty-first-century media at our disposal, why are we losing the battle to capture people's hearts with God's truth? How can we make truth stick?*

One of the Bible storytellers who helped record the Bible stories of *Following Jesus* gave me the clue I was looking for. Steve Evans said: "An oral learner enters the story. He is *inside* it. A literate learner stands outside the story and evaluates it."[1]

I had a flashback to my childhood when I listened to the Lone Ranger radio program every day.[2] I was *inside* those stories. I rode with the Lone Ranger and Tonto. I heard the hoofbeats of the horses and experienced the bad guys attacking us. These things were as real to me as if I were there.

When I shared this experience with a media group, a man responded, "That's true. My children loved 'Adventures in Odyssey' by Focus on the Family as a radio drama, but they were very disappointed when the videos came out. Their imaginations were far richer than what the filmmakers could put on video."

INVOLVED IN THE ACTION

So why are Bible stories not as real to us? After all, they really happened at one time and are not just the product of some author's imagination. How do we bring the Bible to life in the twenty-first century? I believe we do it by involving people in the Bible story—by letting them vicariously live the Bible story in such a way that they relate it to their own stories. Good stories can engage our imaginations so that a movie plays in our minds. We identify with the characters in the story and enter their world. Stories can evoke personal emotions and help us enter a virtual three-dimensional world that our minds create. As we relive an event told from God's Word, it plays with power and conviction in our heads—and hearts.

Imagining a good story makes it as real as if we're *there*. We can stop the story at any time and mull over a specific point. Effortlessly we rocket through our memories and think of a time when something similar happened to us as it did to biblical characters: nearly drowning in a lake, getting too close to a superheated furnace, standing on top of a high building, being too sick to stand, holding the lifeless body of a child and weeping through the loss . . . whatever is relevant. We can instantaneously return to the story without a glitch. That is the power of our God-given imaginations!

I learned much of what we are calling the TruthSticks strategy of Bible storying from my eight mentors in the *Following Jesus* group and through my personal experiences of storying around the world over the past ten years. Our goal is to bring the Bible to the lives and lips of His people.

GET PEOPLE INTO THE BIBLE

I use three kinds of hooks to engage listeners with the Bible story. A question mark is like a hook (?), while an exclamation mark acts like a club (!). I like to hook my audience with questions instead of beating them over the head with information. Hooks are used to catch onto things—in Velcro, in fishing, and in life. I will discuss three ways of fishing to illustrate the kinds of hooks I use to introduce a story and engage the participants.

Hook to the Past
My first hook is like the hook on the fishing lure that I cast into the past (if you can visualize me casting the lure back to my right) with a spinning rod. By this, I mean that I ask them questions about the last story in the series. I do this because the Bible is one story with many acts and scenes. I want to link the story I'm about to tell to the storying experience that they had the previous week and have already incorporated into their lives. I ask questions, such as:

- "What did you learn from last week's story?"
- "What happened when you told it to your family, friends, or even strangers?"
- "How did the story affect your behavior?"
- "Did you have any problems when you tried to apply the story to real life?"
- "Do you have any questions about the story?"

Using these questions, I reach back to a personal shared experience and start a discussion.

Hooked in the Present

The second set of questions is like fly-fishing. Fly fishermen know the "fly" is so light that they have to swish the heavy fishing line back and forth over their heads several times until they can drop the fly with its hook near a log in the river where the trout are lurking. The questions or situations I introduce with the second hook link the issue in the story I am going to tell with an issue my hearers are facing. In the case of YWAM participants, I knew they were considering where they would serve in the world. I used a powerful short film to highlight the need of 840 unreached people groups in the Middle East and focus their attention on the modern-day situation in the same part of the world to which Jonah went. The video ended with the question "Will you be the one to go to one of these unreached people groups?"

On another occasion I hooked into the needs of a group of businesspeople in Denver by showing them a video clip called "After Hours." In the video a man goes back to his office after hours to work on a project. A female employee is still at work, and after some banter, she tries to seduce him. She tells him they will just have some fun together and no one ever needs to know. Just when she says, "I can make you very happy," I stopped the video and asked my listeners to discuss in groups whether they had ever been involved in such a situation at work or knew someone who had been. That question provoked a lively discussion.

At an appropriate time I interrupted the groups and said, "I want to tell you a Bible story that addresses that same situation. It is the story of Joseph and Potiphar's wife." I had their attention! I had studied the story, so I knew the basic need it answered was sexual temptation, and I had chosen my introductory video and questions to get the participants to discuss the real-life issue. I was "swishing the fly rod back and forth" in their minds between the issue in the Bible and the issue I knew the participants faced until I found a way to get them engaged in the real-life issue the Bible story addressed.

Sometimes I engage people by sharing a personal experience, or I ask them to tell about a personal experience they've had related to the subject we will discuss. Sometimes I use a thought-provoking question or quote. You can use all kinds of experiences to help people get involved in the Bible story you are about to tell so they apply it to their real-life issues. It doesn't have to be profound or elaborate—just real.

Hook to the Future

The third hook is like using a cane fishing pole with a hook or two on a line under a cork bobbing in the water (which I hold to my left). By this, I mean that I ask them a couple of questions so they will listen for the answers as I tell the Bible story. I try to ask questions that set up my audience to look for new information we can relate to future action and life change. In the situation above, when I was introducing the story of Joseph and Potiphar's wife, I asked, "Why do you think Joseph would be vulnerable to seduction?" and "How did Joseph deal with this temptation?" These questions made them active listeners and at the same time focused their attention on answers to their needs that we would discuss.

TELL THE BIBLE STORY

Most of us talk *about* the accounts in the Bible without really telling them *as stories*. We expect people to know the story. But in today's culture, we cannot assume even church members know the Bible stories. Literate communicators usually summarize Bible stories, leaving out all the vivid sensory data that would cause God's truth to stick. The sensory data is all there because the Bible was written for oral-preference people.

When I am talking with small groups, I usually tell the listeners to keep their Bibles closed so they will listen to the story instead of reading it. I do open my Bible (even though I don't look at it) so they will know that the story comes from God's Word and is not made up. This is critical if they can't or don't read, and it reaffirms the source for those who do. I start the story by saying, "Here's the story from God's Word."

TELL THE STORY ACCURATELY

I tell the story as accurately as I can. I don't try to memorize it because that would make it hard to retell for both me and the listeners. It is a story, so I tell it as a story.

Before I learned the storying process, I used to try to modernize Bible stories. For example, I would tell the story of the prodigal son as if it happened recently in a nearby city. People would enjoy the story, but it was not what the Bible said. We are to communicate the Word of God as clearly and accurately as possible; we want those we are discipling to know the difference between the Word of God and our comments about it. For twenty-first-century oral-preference learners, we need to reinforce what God says. For that reason, we do not add anything.

We tell the story in past tense as it is in the Bible. This does two things: It conveys the message the way God intended to communicate it, and it is simple enough that anyone can repeat it. We do not teach what the story means. That's hard for those of us who are teachers and preachers because we like to add our comments or salient insights while we are telling the story. We want to tell people our understanding of the background or our interpretation of the facts. But there is a better way to get them involved in the truth than telling them what the story means; we'll explore that in the next chapter.

Stories from the Heart

Most of the Bible stories I know came from my grandmother. Every winter my parents went on a two-week vacation, and my brother and I stayed with Mimi, our grandmother. As part of getting us ready for bed, my grandmother pulled the shades, turned out the lights, and told us a Bible story. No Bibles were present in that dark room; we couldn't have read them anyway. *She* was our Bible, and she wouldn't tell anything except Bible stories. We never let her tell just one. Throughout my childhood, my brother and I must have heard hundreds of stories from her.

And Mimi knew her Bible! I never remember her reading anything other than her Bible. When she told the stories, she never stumbled. They flowed from her with seemingly little effort. She brought the Bible to life, and I humbly appreciate the heritage she poured into my life.

Ultimately, Mimi got us to fall in love with the Lord. Because she had a bond with the Lord to begin with, it shaped every intonation, every syllable, and every ounce of her being. Sometimes she would cry — and we'd cry too. Our emotions and reactions were real because she cared enough to make the stories real. Those stories made God's truth stick in our hearts.

— Mark

It thrills me to use Bible stories because I am actually telling people the *Bible*. I don't tell them some scholar's viewpoint or describe an ivory-tower argument. I let the Bible speak directly to them instead of depending on others' interpretations. The Holy Spirit interprets and applies the Bible to people's lives when we engage them with questions. They come up with questions and insights I have never thought of. I don't always know the answers to their questions, but that makes everyone search even more.

Jim Harris, one of the pastors at Real Life Ministries in Post Falls, Idaho, said, "For years we used a home-group curriculum based on the pastor's sermon, and usually only two or three even brought their Bibles. Since we introduced Bible storying, everyone brings their Bibles!"[3] First, they want to check to be sure what the storyteller shares is in the Bible. Second, they want to understand what God meant by that story.

IMAGINING THE STORY

So where does imagination come in? We use our imaginations as we prepare, by recreating the story in our minds so we can tell it as accurately as possible. Our listeners will use their imaginations to do the same thing. Both of us are building on the Word of God and using our own images and experiences to remember it. We imagine both the environment and the situation where the story takes place. We imagine the scene alive with colors, sounds, smells, and tastes. We put ourselves in the place of the main characters. Every person in the story has a story. If we are telling the story of Jesus healing the blind man by spitting in his eyes, we can imagine the blind man's feelings (see Mark 8:22-26). We can ask ourselves questions such as "Why did Jesus choose to heal him that way?"

Imagine the reactions of different characters in the story. Close your eyes and imagine what life must have been like for the people in the Bible story. What would you have needed to carry with you that day? Where would you have lived? How would you have encountered the persons in the story? The "theater of the mind" clearly outdistances the single viewpoint of a movie. This will not only prepare you to tell the story interestingly, but it will also help you to know which questions to ask during the dialogue time. You may want to do some research about the historical context and culture so you are accurate in your descriptions.

BE YOURSELF

Let your own personality shine through when you tell the story. Don't overdramatize it or tell it in a monotone. Some people are naturally more dramatic than others, but anyone can tell a story. If you don't think so, ask a fisherman about the last big fish that got away or a grandmother about her new granddaughter. Be yourself.

You want to tell the story to the group in such a way that they can turn around and share this story with others. Steve Douglass, president of Campus Crusade for Christ, likes to say that most speakers want to hear other people tell them how good their speech was, as if to say, "I wish I could speak like that." Then he adds with a twinkle in his eye, "But if you want them to reproduce themselves and start a movement, you would rather hear them say, 'That was pretty good, but I can do that.'"[4]

LEARNING THE STORY

How do we remember the story? Here are some tools I have found effective. Read the passage aloud over and over using a modern-language version so it sounds more natural. After reading the story several times, try telling it out loud. Check the Bible to see what you have left out or added. Record yourself telling the story and listen to it on your MP3 player. Imagine the story as it unfolds before you as if you were watching a movie or video.

Picture the drama unfolding through the characters of the story. Plot out the actions in the story, because actions make a story live. Imagine what the various characters in the story are doing, thinking, seeing, hearing, and feeling. Ask yourself how they are interacting with the other characters. Think of the locations in the story and how you can move around on an imaginary stage. John Walsh likes to story-board the story, so he draws stick figures to remind him of each scene. Don't tell your audience what you are imagining, because that would be adding to the story; they will sense the drama of the story from your words and actions. Try telling the story over and over to yourself and to family members or friends. One man from Springdale, Arkansas, told everyone who came into his auto tire store the story he was learning to tell to his small group. You inhabit the story so the hearers can get inside it with you.

Concluding the Story — With a Difference

After I told the businesspeople the story of Joseph and Potiphar's wife, I closed my Bible and said, "That's the story from God's Word. Now let's talk about it." You can tell most Bible stories in five to ten minutes. If the story takes longer than that, you probably need to break it up into smaller segments to tell on different occasions, as I did with the Joseph account.

So what's the big deal? Haven't most of us heard these stories multiple times? The difference is that if you have really learned the story by heart, you own it and it shows. If you look people in the eye as you tell it, they realize you really think the story is important and they should listen. If you have set up the story to speak to the listeners' needs using the process outlined above, almost everyone will be glad to hear your story.

Getting the Bible into Them

I learned that interactive dialogue is where the Bible really comes to life for most people. My puzzle was beginning to make sense.

Getting the Bible story inside people is so important that we will spend the entire next chapter discussing how to ask the right questions following the telling of the story—questions that will hook God's truth into their hearts. Future chapters will explore the other elements I used with YWAM to show how to engage people with drama, song, and poetry. In the following chapter, however, we will consider how to stir up our creative, memory-making juices by asking the right questions following the story.

QUESTIONS FOR REFLECTION

1. Think of a favorite Bible story and ask yourself, "Why it is a favorite story?"
2. Think of one of God's truths and identify several Bible stories in which that truth is communicated. What hooks could you use to get people involved in the main truth or issue in the story?
3. What is the difference between reciting a memorized story and telling a story?
4. How alive and practical is the Bible for you? How could you use stories to get inside the Bible and get the Bible inside of you?

HEAD, HEART, HANDS

A certain rich Texan left a will for his three children. The lawyer read the will, which said, "God has been good to me, and I want to share His blessings with you, my beloved children. I had to discover the blessings of God. I will give you the same privilege. Each of you will receive a ten-square-mile section of land in a different part of Texas, and you will find your treasure there if you look for it." After designating who had each piece of land, their father wished them God's speed.

The three children were dismayed that they would not receive their inheritance immediately. They asked the lawyer to tell them the secret of where the treasure was buried. He said he did not know.

John, the first son, searched his land with a metal detector but found only parts of old farm instruments. The second son, James, tried a divining fork on his land and found an underground stream. The daughter, Jenny, got her jeans smeared with the tar that oozed from a section of her land but saw no indications of treasure.

A month later the three adult children called a meeting to see what they had discovered. John, James, and Jenny all had similar stories of not finding anything of value. They were ready to give up when the lawyer reminded them that their father loved them and assured them he had left treasure for each of them if they would look for it.

In time Jenny moved to the city, complaining that her father had made it too confusing to find her inheritance. But John and James decided their father loved them and it would be worth whatever it cost to find their treasure. Over the next few years John developed a very productive farm where he had discovered parts of farm instruments. James discovered an artesian well that fed the stream on his land, and he developed a business supplying bottled water. Jenny and her husband went about their own business and never found their treasure. They left their empty land to their children, never realizing that a vast oil field lay untapped.

Jesus told a similar story of a man who found buried treasure in a field; he sold everything he had and bought the land where the treasure was still buried (see Matthew 13:44). God our Father has filled His Word with treasures, many of them hidden in stories. This chapter shows you how to use questions to help small-group members dig out the treasure of His truth that God put in stories. Since some people have difficulty asking the right kind of questions, I will give more practical help in this chapter.

JESUS' USE OF QUESTIONS

Jesus was not only the Master Storyteller but also the Master Questioner. He asked questions before, during, and after His stories and teachings.

He interjected them directly into the course of conversations. The stories He told posed internal questions for His listeners, even when not asked directly. The questions, stories, and parables were intentionally designed to create a response. Jesus used questions to expose error and reveal deeper truths. To Jesus, the crucial questions dealt with attitudes, relationships, value judgments, and heart responses. Jesus pushed toward a deeper understanding that touched the heart and soul and brought spiritual transformation. To get a clearer understanding of Jesus' use of questions, observe how He used questions in the Gospels.

GETTING THE BIBLE INTO PEOPLE

When we finish telling the story, we are less than halfway through the storying session. In the previous chapter we talked about how to get people into the Bible; in this chapter we will concentrate on how to get the Bible into them. As storytellers and facilitators of small-group learning, how can you use questions to help people discover the treasures God has put in the Bible stories?

Most people discover these treasures during the interactive discussion time that we call *dialogue*. A story puts everyone on the same level because anyone can talk about a story and what it means. That is why parable-oriented books such as *Who Moved My Cheese* work so well in business and why business schools like Harvard primarily use case studies in their MBA programs. I am amazed how people will discuss a Bible story when they would be terrified to give a speech about it. Dialogue brings the Bible to life.

THREE KINDS OF QUESTIONS

Questions allow listeners to take ownership of what they have heard and make personal discoveries. Questions help unlock the heart and the head on the way to activating the hands and feet in application.[1]

We looked at three kinds of questions to use in the introduction of the story in the previous chapter. Now let's look at how to ask three other basic kinds of questions in the dialogue that follows the story. These dialogue questions deal with our heads (knowledge), our hearts (emotions/wills), and our hands (actions) and can be remembered in several ways. Pick the set of prompts that best suits you from any of the horizontal lines in the chart below.

THE QUESTIONS CHART

HEAD	HEART	HANDS
What?	Why?	How?
What?	So what?	Now what?
Observations	Implications/ Interpretation	Application

The first row in the chart above focuses on the target for the questions, and every column under it is another way to remember the same kind of questions you ask about each. Choose the row that is the easiest to remember. Pastors may recognize that the last row describes the functional elements of preaching. In preaching classes "observations" is often called "explanation" since the preacher is telling people what he has observed in the text. However, in the story dialogue sessions we do not tell people what the story means. Instead we ask the participants to come up with the sequence of events in the story as well as the answers to questions.

One participant in a storying workshop I led kept pressing his group to give the answer he obviously wanted. During the debrief of the session I told him, "You are not the message; the story is the message. You are to ask questions so that they can discover the truth in the story rather than you pushing your ideas on them." In addition, if they discover the message themselves, as opposed to being forced into it, they will remember it better.

God's truth is in the story, but you have to gently open it up with questions to make it come alive for the group. When we use good questions, ordinary participants often come up with insights that even the commentaries leave out.

QUESTIONS THAT FOCUS ON UNDERSTANDING

Use the questions in the sidebar by Don Falkos, who frequently coaches storytellers at the International Orality Network conferences, to help you personally learn the story and understand it. Then use the same questions to prepare yourself to craft questions for the interactive dialogue.

Questions to Help You Understand the Story

Who is in the story?
Name all the characters, whether they are people, animals, or something else altogether.

What is in the story?
Name all objects, large and small.

Where does the story take place?
Describe the setting of the story. Consider things such as the country, city/town, neighborhood, street, structure, room, field, lake, cave, and so on. Include the climate. Weather conditions are part of the setting.

When does the story take place?
Identify the time frame of the story. Consider the era, year, season, month, day, and time of day. How does the time frame of this story relate to other historical events? Consider the time span. How long does it take for the events to unfold?

What is the problem?
Identify any problem, obstacle, barrier, or difficulty presented in the story.

What happens?
Recount the events of the story in the order they occur.

What is the resolution?
Is the problem solved? Is the obstacle, barrier, or difficulty overcome? If so, how?[2]

— Don Falkos

After you discover the truths yourself using the questions in the sidebar, design questions that will help the participants discover the truth. Dennis Stokes, national training director, and Ralph Ennis, director of intercultural training and research, both with The Navigators, have spent years learning to ask the right questions. Ralph said,

An underlying goal is to get members to talk to one another. The facilitator isn't just answering a question back and forth like ping-pong. Get the group to talk to each another. When one person dominates the discussion, open the discussion back up by asking someone else's opinion. When someone asks you a question, ask for answers from the group or say, "What do you think?" If you can't get them talking back and forth to each other, look down. It forces them to look at someone else.[3]

Head Questions

You ask *head* questions to help your listeners remember the facts of the story in sequence. By asking what happened in the story first, second, third, and so on, you help them mentally review the story and remember what happened when. Involve the entire group in reconstructing the story. If they respond with an event or dialogue out of sequence, ask the group what happened before that incident occurred. If someone leaves out an item, ask others to help the group remember each thing in the correct order. As they rebuild the story, ask them to repeat what each character said.

Most groups get extremely engaged because you are asking easy fact questions—*head* questions—about what they have just heard. Usually a group can rebuild the story in ten minutes or less, but it is important not to skip this step. Inexperienced facilitators often let the group move too quickly to application (*hand* questions). If you move too quickly to interpretation or application questions (*heart* questions), the participants may clam up. Getting the Bible story inside their heads prepares them to get it deeper in their hearts and put it into practice with their hands. A variation of this exercise is to ask the group to tell the story, with each person sharing a different part and the group correcting itself.

Heart Questions

Heart questions deal with implications and interpretations of the story; they enable the listeners to understand what the story means. Use open-ended questions that require more than one-word answers. Use questions that cause them to think, to wonder, and to reflect on the motives of the people in the story. Use "why" questions or "so what" questions. Ask questions that don't have obvious answers so the audience can't guess what you're looking for as an answer. Don't ask yes or no questions.

Here are some simple interpretation questions that you can use with any scripture. A pastor in Indonesia I was discipling asked how to help members of his new church start home Bible groups. I gave the following questions to ten of his church members, and they started ten home groups. The pastor reported to me later that some groups would stay up most of the night talking about the answers to these questions.

I have listed them and added hand signs to help you remember them.

 What does this story tell us about God? (Point your index finger upward.)

 What does this story tell us about humans? (Point your index finger downward.)

 Did you see anything new to you in this story? (Put your thumb to your temple and flip your hand up with your fingers extended.)

 Do you have a question about anything in the story? (Lift your hands and shrug your shoulders.)

 What does this story say we should do? (Point your index finger toward the individuals in the group.)

Other questions could include: "What do you like about this story?" and "What don't you like about this story?" Guide the interactive dialogue with questions that help the group members interpret the story. Involve the group in answering the questions.

The most difficult thing for teachers and preachers to overcome in this process is the habit of interjecting their explanations during the telling of the story or the dialogue. Many of us fear that ordinary people won't interpret the story correctly, or we just want to tell them what we know. Remember when you tell Bible stories, do not tell the listeners *your* interpretation of the story; you are responsible for guiding them to biblical interpretations.[4] If the answer to your question or theirs is not clear from the story, ask if they know other stories that shed light on the problem. If someone gives an answer that is not correct, get the group to discuss the options and lead them to the best interpretation. If no one knows the answer to a question, say that you will try to find the answer by the next meeting. Unless you need to head off heresy, let the members help you lead the group to an accurate interpretation. If they don't, you may speak up and give your interpretation or tell the person you will talk with him or her after the session.

Hand Questions

You want to move beyond interpretation to application and transformation. That's the purpose of *hand* questions. Stokes and Ennis pointed out that Jesus was always seeking deeper things. "When we look at the stories of Jesus with His audiences, what was He hoping they would conclude?" asked Dennis. "In the parables of Christ, He wanted the Pharisees and others to grapple with their view of God. He was uncovering their relationships with others that pointed to their relationship with God."[5]

In this application section ask the group, "What should we do differently this week because of this story?" Get the group to agree on one way to apply the story that week and report back the following meeting. Members may mention individual applications and ask the group to hold them accountable by checking how they are doing.

DIFFERENT QUESTIONS FOR DIFFERENT PERSONALITIES

Remember, certain people's personalities come alive depending on what type of story you tell them and what type of questions you ask. What is a strategic question for one person may be a frustrating question for another. Vary the category of questions you ask; if you are aware of specific personality types in your group, ask them specific types of questions to be more effective.

Martin Deacon taught DiSC-related team and relationship seminars for Walk Thru the Bible for many years.[6] He said that most of the time we use questions that catch people like ourselves but fail to engage people with different personalities. Here are his suggestions on how to ask questions for people who have a different learning orientation than you.

The social extroverts want to be asked, period! They love to talk; they need little prompting and respond intuitively. Give them opportunities to express themselves without letting them take over the whole discussion. They like to answer the "who" type questions. Let them share how the story relates to their lives. Be enthusiastic with them and affirm them appropriately. Disagree with grace when necessary, and ask for other opinions without shaming them.

The socially calm or reserved persons may be shy and unwilling to share with the whole group. Create a safe environment, and do not put them on the spot; perhaps give them time to first relate to a smaller group or the person next to them. Also let them discover or talk about the "why" and reflect on the reason the story is included or why the characters said or did what they did. Affirm them without focusing unwanted attention on them.

The people who are investigators want to reflect on the details and not miss anything. Be sure to ask them the "how" type questions and inquire about other details in the story—this motivates them. They will help the group to stay accurate. They do not want to be rushed, so give them time to reflect and correct the group. You may want to remember they fear being wrong or criticized, so they need time and grace.

Task-oriented persons usually want to discover what difference the story makes in their own lives—or the lives of others. Make sure to ask them "what" questions as well as the "so what" questions. Remember that they tend to get bored if a discussion gets too long or does not move toward a conclusion. They want to apply what they've discovered, so ask them questions that challenge them to action.

MAKE IT PRACTICAL

In a home group at Real Life Ministries, the leader told the story about Jesus asking Peter to launch out into the deep water and then to follow Him and "catch men" (see Luke 5:1-11). During the interactive dialogue the leader asked the members what they would be doing if they had been at the Sea of Galilee the day Jesus got into Peter's boat.

An eight-year-old boy who was there with his grandfather said, "I'd be skipping rocks." But he listened intently to the story and the entire dialogue. When they got home, the boy arranged three chairs in his upstairs room and called, "Grandpa, come up to my room. I have something to tell you." He told him the story just as he had heard it and then imitated the leader and asked, "What do we learn about God in this story? What do we learn about people? What should we do because of this story?"

His grandfather noticed how the room was set up and asked, "What is this other chair for?"

The boy responded, "I am going to learn another story next week, and I think I have friends who would like to hear my stories."

Bible storying is reproducible even by children, and questions make it work.

Asking questions like these can seem simplistic, but I am surprised how relevant they are. Also, I have discovered that I can go beyond these basic questions into the meaning of the passage—as deep as I desire—by asking insightful questions. If you ask the right kind of questions, you will probably have to call a halt after an hour or so. Why? Because the people will be so interested in exploring the story and interpreting why the story happened as it did, what it means, and how they can apply the truths to their everyday lives.

These basics of storying filled in the pattern of the puzzle I was trying to put together. However, to make disciples, we'll see in the next chapter that storying in the midst of face-to-face relationships provides a human network to bring the puzzle together.

QUESTIONS FOR REFLECTIONS

1. What is the difference between a hook and a club when it comes to communicating God's Word?
2. What are the advantages of drawing out God's truth through dialogue instead of telling it to those in a small-group setting?
3. Try these questions for the story of the prodigal son:
   a. What are some *head* questions you could ask that would contribute to knowledge?
   b. What are some *heart* questions you could ask to surface emotions?
   c. What are some *hands* questions you could ask to bring about action?

CHAPTER 6

FACE-TO-FACE

Come with me to visit a small-group meeting in a high-rise apartment. One of the participants, Candice, has just told her first Bible story and led the dialogue.

She lets out a sigh of relief, even though the story really seemed to flow. As people listened, it was if they were *there*. They were caught up in the story. One young mother dabbed tears from her eyes with a tissue. The discussion time following the story is especially lively. Derek, the small-group leader, compliments Candice on her preparation and delivery, and he encourages her to become a regular at telling stories. In fact, he pulls out his calendar and schedules her to tell another Bible story in two weeks.

Candice smiles and agrees. She knows that something special has happened, but she doesn't have a clue what made it so unique. While the group is getting ready to leave, Candice asks, "Derek, was this a fluke? What if I'm a flop next time?"

"You were faithful to prepare and lead this session, and the Holy Spirit blessed!" Derek replies. "Here are two ways that I saw Him at work tonight. Our group has created a safe environment where the Bible can come alive. There's trust here."

"And love, too," adds Candice. "We have really discovered something more precious than TV shows or other time robbers. This face-to-face time has really become a priority to us."

"That didn't happen overnight," Derek says.

"True. It has been coming together for several months. There's a hunger growing to really hear God's Word in fresh ways. Everyone was pulling for me. That helped encourage me!"

"There you go. We've got a relational environment that is very supportive. The Bible story that you told was eagerly welcomed," points out Derek. "What a blessing!"

"So, the secret is to have good relationships and be supportive, right?" asks Candice.

"That was one of the two things I had in mind," says Derek with a smile.

"I thought there might be something else, but other than you getting me to tell another story in two weeks, I don't have a clue."

"There, you did it."

"Did what? I'm a little confused." Candice's face is puzzled.

"There you go again."

"Do you mean that I'm honest about my inadequacies?" she blurts out.

"Exactly," Derek says. "You're transparent about your worries, but you feel accountable to the Lord, me, and our group about your next assignment."

"Well, yes, otherwise none of us would make much progress. We are a group that's willing to share our failures as well as our successes. The accountability that we have with each other is what makes the difference, isn't it?"

"You've got it, Candice," Derek says.

"Supportive relationships and transparent accountability!" Candice smiles.

Churches are discovering the importance of face-to-face relationships to personalize God's Word. Becoming more relational by being supportive of each other and then being transparent enough to be held accountable—these things are possible in the real world. And I saw them firsthand—in northern Idaho!

REAL LIFE MINISTRIES

One day I got a phone call from Marcus Vegh—yep, the same guy who started me on my quest of discovering how to make disciples of oral learners when I was in Amsterdam. He had moved to Coeur d'Alene, Idaho, and had become an elder at Real Life Ministries in Post Falls, ten miles away. He told me excitedly about his church. I couldn't figure out what was different about it until I met his pastor, Jim Putman. Marcus invited Jim to a Finishing the Task Conference where I spoke about using oral strategies overseas. Later Jim phoned me and said, "I think that is what we need for our small groups in our church. Could you come teach us about making disciples using Bible stories?"

I was intrigued because Real Life Ministries had already grown to thousands in attendance while my denomination's experience in Idaho had been that churches usually topped out at around a hundred and fifty members.

MORE THAN A COINCIDENCE

At that time, I was so focused on leading the International Orality Network to influence the body of Christ to make disciples of the world's four billion oral learners that I didn't think I had time to worry about the United States. My friends and I had experienced phenomenal breakthroughs in making God's truth stick in oral cultures. Could those same oral strategies work in churches whose members were used to having books, workbooks, fill-in-the-blanks studies, and video curricula at their fingertips?

I wondered, *Is God offering me the opportunity to try a pilot project in the United States among oral-preference learners—people who can read but prefer to get information through oral and visual means? How can I apply what I have been learning about biblical discipleship in oral cultures to America's oral-preference culture? Is this church another piece of the puzzle that God is putting together?*

When Jim Putman described his disciple-making commitment and passion for churches in America to make disciples, I sensed God saying, "Go for it!" As I made my way to Post Falls, I wondered (tongue in cheek), *Can anything good come out of Post Falls, Idaho?* Was I in for a surprise!

A NEW WAY TO LOOK AT CHURCH

Jim Putman had been a champion wrestler in high school and college. He developed a very successful coaching career while serving as part-time youth director at his church in Oregon.

Then two couples from Post Falls asked him to move there and start a church. He told them his personal opinions about church, which were shaped by his sports background. Jim believed that the pastor was a coach who helped the members play the game. He was not the player, and they were not just spectators. Instead, it was the other way around—they were the players, and he was the coach. He told the couples that he believed the church's number one priority was to make disciples, and he would lead the whole church to make disciples if he started the church with them. They would make disciples in relational small groups shepherded by church members.

TRANSFORMATIONAL SMALL GROUPS

The new church first met in the home of one of the couples. It quickly outgrew that space, moved into the garage, then to a nearby theater, and after that to a school gymnasium. In four years the church had 2,300 people attending and had built a building. None of the leaders, including Jim, had ever been in a church with more than three hundred members. These leaders did not start out nor expect to build a megachurch; they just wanted to make disciples and change the world one person at a time!

God was up to something. But in the midst of the growth, Real Life Ministries faced a crisis. Jim came into the office exhausted in the middle of the week. One of the staff members asked, "What's up with you?"

"I have made 162 phone calls to absent members this week."

"Why are you doing that?"

"Why wouldn't I? I am the shepherd, and when a sheep is lost, why wouldn't you go after him?"

The whole staff gathered around and replied, "There are too many people now for you to do it alone. We all have to pitch in and help. Your job is to make sure people are shepherded. You always talk about raising up people to do what you do; now let us do what you do."

On Sunday, Jim described the crisis to the church. He lined up all the staff in front of the church. He laid everything out. He told them how stretched the staff members were. How they were headed for burn-out. How they were convinced that they had to focus on developing disciples more than investing in a well-crafted worship "show." They would put their money into disciple-making leaders.

The response was amazing! Jim said, "We shared the plan. We would become completely small groups driven. . . . We let them know they would have to step up and become ministers, not spectators—after all, this church is called Real Life Ministries, and we must all be ministers. The people went nuts. They gave us a standing ovation! In two weeks we grew another five hundred people."[1]

SMALL-GROUP DISCIPLESHIP

The small-group leaders began to truly shepherd their multigenerational home groups. Small-group discipleship became the fundamental DNA of Real Life Ministries, influencing everything they did and shaping how the church grew. On my first visit I discovered that the groups echoed real life. The leaders and the members were transparent about their struggles and failures. Small-group members cared about each other and developed deep personal relationships. They helped people with real-life issues. They held each other accountable and supported and encouraged each other.

I consulted with the church leaders one week every quarter over the next three years. We showed the leaders how they could incorporate Bible storying into the discipleship process. The pastor didn't want to upset their growth by introducing change too quickly, and during the first year the staff tried it out in the small groups they led. By the second year the rest of the small-group members and their leaders were clamoring to know more about what the people in the staff-led small groups were talking about. The home groups began Bible storying churchwide in the fall of the second year, and they told thirty-four stories from creation to Christ during the nine-month school year. The same year they started telling Bible stories, they also shifted from relational groups to geographic groups—and the number of home groups grew 25 to 30 percent![2]

For the third year I proposed that the leaders tell the stories of Jesus' encounters with the disciples chronologically, to see what we would learn about both becoming and making disciples. I recorded *Following Jesus Together*, thirty-four stories for the storytellers to listen to so they could learn them more easily. Jim Blazin, home-groups pastor, asked me questions, and I gave tips from the same stories for leaders on how to make disciples.[3]

USING BIBLE STORYING IN SMALL GROUPS

When I taught the staff to use Bible storying in their small groups, Brandon Guindon, now executive pastor of Real Life Ministries, was the small-groups pastor. He wasn't sold on Bible storying, but he thought he'd give it a try. Brandon recounted,

> I told the story of the fall of man. I was real nervous because I had always led a small group using a curriculum. I liked that structure. I overprepared and tried to memorize the story too much. But when we jumped into the story, I noticed something right off the bat that I had never seen before. People were engaged. They were sitting forward in their chairs. And what amazed me was [that] people were listening like they had never heard the story, although I knew they had because we had studied it before.
>
> When I began to ask them to tell the story back to me, people who never spoke up before began to answer, and then the whole group got involved. I sat there almost as an observer while the group self-corrected itself on the story. To be honest with you, it was somewhat frustrating. I said, "It can't be this easy. I've spent all these years working with curriculum." It was incredible to me to watch how effective it was.
>
> Then a single gal in the group who has three boys and was

usually pretty quiet really got engaged and told more of the story than anyone else. I asked the questions about what we learn about God and man, but when I got to the question on how we could apply this story, I looked over at her and she was crying. I stopped the group, wondering what I had said wrong, and one of the other gals asked Terri what was wrong. She said, "For the first time, I feel like I can go home and teach the Bible to my boys. Can I tell this story to them?" Of course we said she could. So she said, "Then I can disciple my children."[4]

This experience sold Brandon on storying as a way to make disciples.

THE MOOSE CALL

What makes the small-group times so powerful is the relational concern the members have for one another. One night just as Brandon was leaving a seminar where he was training visiting pastors, he got a call from the wife of a man who had not returned from moose hunting. The couple were new Christians and had just come into his group. Although Brandon was tired when he answered the phone that night, he knew he had to go find the husband. Then the phone rang again, and it was the husband. "Brandon, I got my first moose, but I don't know how to cut this two-thousand-pound monster up and get him to the truck." He sounded desperate.

Although Brandon had to teach at eight o'clock the next morning, he called some of his group members, and they set out to find the lost husband and the moose. It took two or three hours to cut up the moose and cart him back to the truck. It was three thirty in the morning when Brandon rode home in the truck with this new Christian. He was a tough guy, but Brandon noticed that he was crying.

"What's wrong?" Brandon asked.

"Now I understand what church is. You were the church to me

tonight!" he sobbed. The people at Real Life Ministries are living out the DNA of first-century discipleship to bring people into face-to-face relationships in a small group.

EXPONENTIAL GROWTH

In ten years Real Life Ministries has grown to more than eight thousand in attendance in worship and about seven thousand involved in small-group discipleship, even though Post Falls has a population of about twenty-five thousand people. These numbers are impressive, but even more gratifying is that the people who are coming to Christ are becoming real disciples and making disciples.

Real Life Ministries started the initial groups based on friendships. As their homes got crowded, the members soon realized that they needed to branch out and start new groups. Branching is a regular part of Real Life Ministries' growth. As they were moving to use Bible storying, they restructured their small groups into geographical zones. Jim Blazin pointed out that Real Life Ministries is "broken into geographical communities. Our goal—the 'win,' if you will—for our communities is that we really do meet the needs within the community for both believers and nonbelievers. Transparency on a level playing field has translated into a much more dynamic serving-ministry/heart-level process."[5]

Immersion

In June 2009, I had an opportunity to experience Immersion I training at Real Life Ministries for staff members from other churches. Anything called *immersion* does not sound like a lecture—and this wasn't. For the most part it was all about experiential learning with fifty church leaders broken into four small groups for the two-day event. The facilitators only presented information for about fifteen minutes, and then each group would spend an hour with two Real Life Ministries staff members facilitating how to apply it to their lives and their particular churches.

We attended a home group one night and a worship service the next. As a storying trainer, I followed up with one of the two full-time Immersion staff, Todd Winslow. He said, "It's interesting to get the perspective from those attending this training who say storying is completely new to them. For those, we find that they are completely blown away by how effective storying is and, without us pushing it much, they are sold out to the idea of implementing storying in their church and small groups. I personally feel that storying is great, but without the component of intentional relationships, storying becomes just another tool. By itself, it doesn't create disciples."[6]

I interviewed Richard Baker and several others from Trinity Point Church in Easley, South Carolina, who attended the Immersion training. After they returned home, their pastor, Mike Mohler, trained the other leaders in their church over nine weeks. In the first six months after starting to use storying, they went from one formal Sunday school class for adults to a dozen home-based small groups with entire families participating.

Richard pointed out, "Once you get twelve to fifteen participants, you develop an apprentice and train him so he can spin off into a new setting. We've called it 'birthing for a purpose'! You've got a set of people you've gotten close to, but we still need to birth a new group."[7]

— Mark

This multiplication mind-set has facilitated Real Life Ministries' evangelistic growth, and they are keeping the Bible at the center of the newly forming relationships. Without God's truth that sticks, the groups could become just another type of social club.

THE CONTEXT OF DISCIPLING

Contrast what I've described here with your experience in your small group, whether it is a Sunday school class, cell group, home Bible study, or curriculum-based group. How deep are the relationships? Do members really care for each other outside the group time? Are they transparent about their struggles and failures? Are they accountable to each other? Are they making disciples? Is God's truth sticking in real life? All of these characteristics are in the DNA of Real Life Ministries.

Jim Putman, Bill Krause (a teaching pastor from Real Life Ministries), and I were talking with the NavPress team in Colorado Springs about this book when I got an e-mail from a pastor who asked, "How do you make disciples through preaching? I want to write a dissertation on it."

I e-mailed him back. "You don't make disciples through preaching. Trying to make disciples through preaching is like spraying milk over a nursery full of screaming babies just hoping some of it falls into their mouths. That is about all you are doing when you are preaching. You make disciples as Jesus did—in face-to-face relationships in small groups. I am not knocking preaching. I taught preaching. You can teach and inspire through preaching, but discipling is done through personal relationships in small groups and one-to-one."

Real Life Ministries gave us a testing ground for three years and allowed us to validate the importance of making disciples in relational, transparent, supportive small groups whose members hold one another accountable to obey the truth learned in Bible stories. You will discover with us more of their strategies throughout the rest of the book.

Jesus gave Himself every day, seven days a week, to a small group of twelve men and discipled them so they could reproduce the process after He returned to the Father. We must recapture what it means in the twenty-first century to make disciples as Jesus did.

QUESTIONS FOR REFLECTION

1. How do the supportive relationships between participants help make truth stick?
2. How can a small-group leader develop a transparent group that holds members accountable?
3. What role do relationships play in growing and multiplying groups?

CHAPTER 7

TOUCHED TO THE CORE

Bobby Welch has trained thousands of Christians to share their faith. The former pastor of First Baptist Church in Daytona Beach, Florida, does a very dramatic—and even dangerous—depiction of Jesus' parable of the lost sheep. Bobby describes in great detail the value of the ninety-nine sheep in the fold. He walks around the front of the auditorium counting his imaginary sheep. He picks up the count in high drama: "Ninety-seven, ninety-eight, ninety-nine . . . ninety-nine? Ninety-nine?" A look of horror comes over his face. "Only ninety-nine!" He looks around, up, and down. "The hundredth sheep is lost!" he shouts.

Frantic, Bobby runs into the audience, looking from row to row of the church. He quickly sprints up the stairs. Halfway up, he "spies" the lost sheep. He cries out in alarm for the sheep to hold on. "I'm coming!" he shouts. Bobby quickly changes to a soothing voice to calm the unseen sheep. All eyes are on Bobby. He is well behind most of the people, so they have to turn in their seats to follow the action.

The church's worship center has a balcony that is a good treetop's distance above the carpeted concrete floor below. Yet Bobby is still on task. He has spotted his sheep, but it's not yet back in the fold. Very carefully, but with determined purpose, Bobby grabs the railing of the balcony. One leg goes over the edge. The crowd gasps. His other leg is tightly wrapped around the railing. Bobby leans far out over the audience. Murmurs of concern grow louder from the audience. People look for some safety net, but there is nothing. Some men spontaneously stand, ready to rescue this zany pastor from his stunt. With no safety rope and no spotters, Bobby releases one hand from the railing and strains out into the air at the imaginary lost sheep.

With a cry of joy, Bobby yells loudly, "Don't worry, little sheep. I've got you!" Bobby pulls himself back onto the railing and into the balcony. He pantomimes putting the lost sheep on his shoulders and makes his way back down to the front. He places the sheep in the imaginary pen. And with a shout of "One hundred!" the drama ends.

Everyone claps — as much for the emotional punch the action carries as in relief that Bobby didn't fall!

EMPATHETIC EMOTIONS

Did Bobby Welch make his point? Did he have to preach on the meaning of what he did? Did anyone present not understand that a shepherd would go to great lengths to rescue even *one* of his sheep? Each listener needed only to apply the truth.

Bobby's dramatic depiction is more extreme than what most of us would do, but what he did was create empathy. Daniel Pink, author of

A Whole New Mind, defined *empathy* as the ability to imagine yourself in someone else's position and to intuit what that person is feeling. It is the ability to stand in others' shoes, to see with their eyes, and to feel with their hearts. It is something we do pretty much spontaneously, an act of instinct rather than the product of deliberation. But empathy isn't sympathy, which is feeling a compassionate emotion *for* someone else. Empathy is feeling *with* someone else, sensing what it would be like to be that person. It is a stunning act of imaginative derring-do, the ultimate virtual reality—climbing into another's mind to experience the world from that person's perspective.[1]

STICKY EMOTIONS

What we do in a Bible-storying group is not nearly as dramatic as what Bobby Welch did, but the same principles are at work. If you want something to *stick*, you involve the emotions.

Dr. Karim Nader and a team of scientists have been looking into the way the brain remembers and stores our strongest memories. They have learned that when something that happens to us is accompanied by a strong emotion, the adrenal gland releases molecules that etch memories into our brains. When the memory of the incident is called up, the brain also retrieves the emotion. This process gives us warm feelings—over and over again—about times shared with childhood friends, a first kiss, and how we felt on our wedding day. Memories can also drag up terrible feelings about abusive situations or violence, perhaps from an accident.[2]

When emotions are felt, chemicals are released into our bloodstream. They come not only from the brain but also from other organs throughout the body. And after these chemicals circulate in us, it takes awhile for them to dissolve away. Our brains cannot just shut off emotions. The exhilaration of winning a football game or the agony of a divorce does not go away quickly. Scientists believe that chemicals, such as peptides, can flow to every cell in the body, making the circulatory system function as a secondary nervous system. When the peptides are released by emotional stimulation in the brain, every cell is affected. When we recognize that the Lord made us with millions of cells, we understand how we experience an emotional reaction down to the very core of our being.[3]

God made us to experience strong emotions. These can become powerful learning agents. Unfortunately, emotions can also be preyed upon. It should go without saying that you never manipulate emotions for emotions' sake. They need to be genuine emotions that emerge out of learning experiences.

The physical movement connected with drama, dance, choreography in music, or simulation games allows our minds to better comprehend God's truths because they connect with our emotions. After the experience, believers can remember and grow spiritually and are motivated to make lifestyle adjustments.

INVOLVING THE EMOTIONS

How can you use emotions to help people remember the Bible, feel the implications of the stories at the core of their beings, and apply them to their own lives? By engaging the emotions as part of the learning process and integrating the emotional factor into the story.

The simplest way to do this is to ask the group to spontaneously act out the story. People may think this is childish or corny; they may even be self-conscious at first. Assure them that as adults we need to do this to really get inside the story. As a storying facilitator, this is the time for you to take a positive attitude and encourage people to take a part. A basic principle of teaching is that most students learn more effectively by doing—by experience. Tell them that everyone is going to be involved. Ask for volunteers who will portray each character or who will be major props in the story. Then just wait until people volunteer.

If necessary, appoint persons to be each character in the story you just told and have them just say or act out what that character does.

Usually you can ask those who don't have an active role to still play some part in the story. For example, if you tell the story of Adam and Eve, say that everyone else is "on stage" to be one of the animals Adam named. Or when you tell the story of Jonah, say that everyone else is a Ninevite and needs to respond accordingly. You can also use some people in nonspeaking parts. For example, in the Adam and Eve story, ask for one person to be the Tree of Life and another person to be the Tree of the Knowledge of Good and Evil; their roles are to stand there with their arms out like branches, giving visual impact. For the Jonah story, ask one person to be the whale and another to be the vine that grows up over Jonah. You can ask several people to be the wind. The more people you can get involved, the greater the impact. Enlist a narrator to tell the parts of the story that have no dialogue.

Assure them that you aren't expecting them to be perfect, but everyone is to do at least two things: have fun, and come to appreciate and feel what the characters in the story felt. You may want to point out certain locations where the action takes place, but it is usually better to let adults determine their own representation. Sit down and turn them loose to be creative. In unusual cases you may have to prompt someone as to what to say or do next. Normally it is better to be silent and wait until the debriefing to address any issues.

A variation of this creative learning time is to ask people to pantomime the action while you tell the story. In fact, you may try this approach first, in some cases, if your audience seems too self-conscious. Then you can do the fully improvised drama.

You never know how the Holy Spirit will inspire a person. A group of men needed a character to play the "Syrophoenician woman," so one man took off his coat and wrapped it around his head to play the part. When a group of ladies needed a "Lazarus" to be dead in the tomb, one very nicely dressed woman simply volunteered and lay down on the floor.

People are really good sports about this if you create a safe environment for them. It's not about their acting prowess; it's about depicting the Bible story so the truth is more easily understood. This is a vision that others will catch; they will then feel freer to participate, regardless of skill level.

Invariably these spontaneous actors will leave something out or add things in order to be funny or dramatic. After the drama is finished, congratulate them and tell them you want to ask a couple of questions to establish exactly what was in the Bible and what was not. Then ask if anything was left out of the story. Ask if anything was added. You need to do this or some people will confuse the acted-out version with the biblical account. If necessary, ask someone to retell the story or retell it yourself. Repeating the story is essential with primary oral learners but also can be important to oral-preference learners. One college coed kept giving rather strange answers in one group. This girl had a solid Christian background, so her answers were a mystery to the leader. He discovered that she was drawing her responses from VeggieTales instead of the Scriptures!

This dramatic reenactment is important for another reason. It helps fix the story in the listeners' minds, which will make it easier for them to tell the Bible story to someone else at a later time that week.

INVOLVE THE ARTS

The storyteller John Walsh uses a different procedure in BibleTelling training to involve everyone in a larger group in the action.[4] After telling the story, he gets everyone to practice it. He shows them a storyboard that he uses to remember the main scenes. His storyboard is simply a set of cards or posters with stick figures depicting the action in the Bible story. John divides the group into pairs and asks them to use his storyboard to retell the story to each other. Then he asks them in larger groups to describe the locations in the story. He retells the story. At that point he divides them into creative-art groups. One group develops a drama; another works out a pantomime. A third group creates a song, and still another paints pictures of the story. Then he has each group present its production to the whole group. By the time John is finished, his listeners have heard or experienced the story *twelve times.*

CREATE SONGS

If you have time after telling the story, dialoguing about it, and acting it out, you can ask the group to create a song about the story. If you don't have time, you can ask some of them to work on creating a song by the next meeting. Music touches the emotions. If you are involved in creating a song, you will likely remember the story better. If the song has a catchy tune, you will sing it during the following week, and it will help you recall the main point of the story. It can even be a ballad that tells the story or echoes a theme in the story.

I admit I was very skeptical of involving others in making up a song even though I had experienced some cultures that would create several songs for one story. I was on my way to teach Bible storying in Bangladesh when I heard Steve Evans, one of the men who helped record the *Following Jesus* audio series and was traveling with me, say, "Every language has a rhythm, and almost every group has at least one person who is musically inclined." That sounded like another piece of the puzzle I was trying to put together.

After I taught the class in Bangladesh, one man asked me to tell a story in their new small group, which met in an apartment building. We agreed to start with the creation story. I discovered that getting all the details straight for this story is hard. Most people cannot tell you what was created on each day. As I told the story, I asked the group to repeat after me the phrase "And God saw that it was good" each time it occurred. The man who had invited me had warned me about one couple in the group. He said, "The husband never talks, but the wife talks all the time." When I asked questions during the dialogue, the man who had been silent answered more questions than anyone else! He was clearly an oral learner. When I asked someone in the group to retell the story, his wife volunteered. She did an excellent job but got mixed up on what was created on which day. I told her not to worry because I was going to help them learn that part. I was improvising and hoping to come up with something.

I repeated the phrase "And God saw that it was good" as I beat out a rhythm on a table. I asked someone to put it to music. The interpreter did so immediately. After the people sang the catchy phrase several times, we began to make up a verse for each day, naming what God made that day. They sang the verses and refrain over and over. By the time we had finished creating the song, with the children thumping the beat on boxes, many more people had joined us. I asked the group if they could go outside to the men gathered at the gate to sing the song and tell the story. They all assured me they could.

Sometimes people will create a song from scratch. At other times they will make up new lyrics to a melody they already know. Occasionally they will sing a song they already know that emphasizes what is being taught in the story, such as "Zacchaeus Was a Wee Little Man" or "The Wise Man Built His House upon the Rock." If time is short, ask the musically inclined members of the group to create or find a song to match the story during the week.

Singing the Story Home

A few years ago I visited an "oral seminary" in southern Sudan. The Anglican church had asked some of our missionaries to train the young men who had been deprived of an education by the war that has been going on with northern Sudan since 1983. The nineteen students had learned 140 Bible stories and made up four or five songs for each one. Every Friday night a huge crowd of people congregated at the market to hear the new songs and dance in a circle as they sang them. I even danced in the circle as they sang the songs about

Noah's ark and the tower of Babel! The songs opened the door for the students to tell the stories that explained the songs. One student said when he returned to his village, the people kept him up until midnight to hear the stories. Another student said that it was three in the morning before his village heard enough stories to let him go to sleep. Another testified that he told Bible stories all night long. The stories spread on the wings of songs.

On the surface, it may appear that the villagers were just interested in hearing several songs and stories to pass the time. However, these stories were specifically chosen and then linked together to make an impact on several cultural barriers to the gospel. The villagers' tribal taboos were being addressed through the Bible stories.

One student said that while he was telling the stories and singing the songs in his village, a man died. The village custom was for the pallbearers to ask the spirits who was responsible for the person's death. They believed that the spirits would guide them to the house of the person who had put a hex on him through black magic. The student jumped in front of the casket and said, "I know why this man died." When the villagers asked why, he told them the story of Adam and Eve and showed that death was the consequence of sin. The people agreed that was a good answer and buried the dead man without trying to blame someone else. God can use His stories and songs to address the core issues of any people in any context.

— Avery

OTHER WAYS TO CONNECT EMOTIONALLY

We can rely on the Lord to provide insight into the specific emotional triggers among the small-group participants. When the storyteller leader is genuinely excited about the story and is involved emotionally in the story and discussion, that enthusiasm becomes contagious. Sometimes the storyteller serves as a role model by truly "walking the talk," which can be thrilling to watch. For example, a Bible-story dialogue followed by the facilitator telling a personal example of overcoming temptation can make a deep impact. When the storyteller is emotionally attached to the story, others get more involved. Don't fear controversy or differences in opinions; they can also be a good way to involve persons.

Celebrations also provide ways to connect emotionally. It can be as simple as a fist bump or elaborate enough to involve food, music, rewards, and other ways to have fun. Recognizing birthdays or anniversaries is another way to add emotional warmth to any group setting.

Bring the Story to Life

When the focus shifts to making disciples instead of preaching or teaching *at* people, the whole situation changes. Bringing the stories of the Bible to life in a way that involves people's emotions allows them to walk away with God's truth deeply embedded in their hearts. The truth of God's Word will *stick* in their heads and hearts. The Holy Spirit can be counted on to interpret the story for you into the lives of those who are wrestling with the truth.

The point is, we use every means that God has given us to help people experience and learn the Bible.

Now I had another important piece of the puzzle of how to make God's truth stick—God wired us so that our emotions are linked with thought processes. When people are touched to the core of their emotions, they don't forget that experience and all that is tied to it!

QUESTIONS FOR REFLECTION

1. Identify ways you could change your worship service and small-group interaction to give them an emotional punch.
2. How can we allow people to have a genuine emotional experience in small groups without manipulating emotions?
3. How can you express a Bible truth or story that is both emotional and memorable?

CHAPTER 8

THE SWORD OF THE SPIRIT

A nine-year-old boy tried to put a jigsaw puzzle together without success. He was about to give up when his mother asked him, "Do you know what picture is on the puzzle?" He shook his head. "Look on the box lid to see the picture." Only then did he see that the puzzle was the face of Christ. Once he had the image in front of him, he was able to assemble the puzzle in just a few minutes to the cheers of his sisters.

Thus far we have been putting together a puzzle on how to make God's truth stick. Although our emphasis up to now has been on making truth stick, we need to clarify what we mean by truth. It takes more than telling Bible stories, deliberately using our senses, and having good interpersonal relationships to make truth stick. It takes the Holy

Spirit shining His light on the truth. Jesus said, "When he, the Spirit of truth, comes, he will guide you into all truth. . . . He will bring glory to me by taking from what is mine and making it known to you" (John 16:13-14).

THE MISSING S

In chapter 2, I referred to the SUCCESs acronym from Chip and Dan Heath's book *Made to Stick*. In their excellent secular model of elements that cause things to be remembered, they listed the following items:

S—Simple
U—Unexpected
C—Concrete
C—Credible
E—Emotional
S—Stories
s

Their last S was tacked on—just something left over that didn't neatly fit their acronym. They had added it to be able to spell the word *success* correctly and form a memorable acronym; it had no word to go with it! But for believers, the last S is not something just tacked on—for us, it is the powerful witness of the Word of God made alive by the Spirit of God. In fact, we have two words to add for the final S:

S—Scripture and the Spirit

You and I need the supernatural power of the truth and the Spirit to put our puzzle together. Truth gives meaning to all the pieces (see 2 Timothy 3:16-17), and the Spirit gives life (see John 6:63). The Holy Spirit is ultimately the One who makes the truth of the Bible stories stick.

By now I hope you are convinced that God has made us with loops (senses) that help us remember His truth, but I suspect your questions about the hooks of truth have been backing up like traffic on the Santa Monica Freeway. Human loops without the hooks of the Word can be used to remember things that are not true. The loops function best when we go beyond the physical senses and the Holy Spirit hooks us into eternal truth.

WHAT IS TRUTH?

The critical issue in the twenty-first century is raised by Pilate's first-century question, "What is truth?" (John 18:38). Many Christians are still asking Pilate's question. According to surveys by George Barna, "Among all born-again adults, about one-quarter make their moral and ethical choices on the basis of the Bible."[1] Worse yet, "Among those who say they rely on biblical standards and principles as their compass for moral decision making, only half believe that all moral truth is absolute."[2] He summed up his research with, "Ninety-one percent of all born-again adults do not have a biblical worldview; 98 percent of all born-again teenagers do not have a biblical worldview."[3] Remember, this survey only dealt with people who described themselves as born-again believers. It did not include other church members and unbelievers, some of whom believe there is no absolute truth.

TRUTH — THE QUESTION FOR THE AGES

This is not just a modern problem. Moses faced the same situation—God's people had been listening to the Egyptians' stories for four hundred years. The Israelites' view of reality (their worldview) had been shaped by the stories they heard when they were being socialized in both the Hebrew and the Egyptian cultures. They had mixed error with truth. Look how quickly they went back to the idea of the golden calf being a god when Moses spent forty days with God on Mount Sinai. God spoke through Moses to reshape the Israelites' worldview to His truth, and Moses wrote God's truth in the first five books of the Bible. He began with, "In the beginning God created the heavens and the earth" (Genesis 1:1). When "God said," He created everything by His Word.

Truth Before the Ages

Truth first lived in the mind of God before the world was created. God created the entire universe by His Word. God is truth and His Word is truth (see John 17:17). A word can reveal who a person is and what he or she is thinking. The world sprang forth at creation as a revelation of who God is. However, the first humans disobeyed God's Word and were separated from Him, so God began to reveal Himself through His acts. Every name for God in the Old Testament was revealed and confirmed through an actual experience. For example, God revealed Himself by the name *Jehovah Jireh*, "God the Provider," when He provided a ram for Abraham's sacrifice in place of his son Isaac. God also revealed truth through His spoken words to holy men who recorded them.

Incarnate Word

When the fullness of time came, God revealed Himself to us by showing up in person: The Word became flesh. "In the beginning was the Word, and the Word was with God, and the Word was God. He was with God in the beginning. Through him all things were made" (John 1:1-3). Jesus not only created the world by the Word but also spoke God's Word to us. The writer of Hebrews said it this way:

> In the past God spoke to our forefathers through the prophets
> at many times and in various ways, but in these last days he
> has spoken to us by his Son, whom he appointed heir of all

things, and through whom he made the universe. The Son is the radiance of God's glory and the exact representation of his being, sustaining all things by his powerful word. (Hebrews 1:1-3)

THE WRITTEN WORD

God revealed reality through both His spoken and incarnate Word, Jesus. "All things were created by him and for him. He is before all things, and in him all things hold together" (Colossians 1:16-17).

God revealed His perfect truth to us as the Holy Spirit moved men to write down His revelation for all generations. Peter summed up God's revelation with his experience with Christ on the Mount of Transfiguration and with God's revelation through the words the prophets wrote under the direction of the Holy Spirit.

We did not follow cleverly invented stories when we told you about the power and coming of our Lord Jesus Christ, but we were eyewitnesses of his majesty. For he received honor and glory from God the Father when the voice came to him from the Majestic Glory, saying, "This is my Son, whom I love; with him I am well pleased." We ourselves heard this voice that came from heaven when we were with him on the sacred mountain.

And we have the word of the prophets made more certain, and you will do well to pay attention to it, as to a light shining in a dark place, until the day dawns and the morning star rises in your hearts. Above all, you must understand that no prophecy of Scripture came about by the prophet's own interpretation. For prophecy never had its origin in the will of man, but men spoke from God as they were carried along by the Holy Spirit. (2 Peter 1:16-21)

USE THE SWORD OF THE SPIRIT

We are usually not trying to defend God's truth when we tell stories to oral-preference learners. Our job is to communicate God's Word and to let the Word itself be its own defense. Paul said, "Take . . . the sword of the Spirit, which is the word of God" (Ephesians 6:17). Can you imagine a Roman soldier trying to verbally defend his sword to an attacking enemy? He could say, "Watch out! A master craftsman made this sword long ago of the finest iron. All the impurities were burned out over a white-hot fire, and it was beaten to shape it into an awesome weapon. I personally sharpened it last night. The edge is sharp enough to peel an apple. The tip is hard enough to penetrate your shield. The handle is strong enough to withstand your weight when I lift you over my head in triumph." No, he doesn't *defend* the sword; he uses it. The truth of the Word proves itself authoritative when we use it.

It has been a special joy to me in the past ten years to tell Bible stories and help people engage directly with the truth. I am not telling these stories as my own opinions or what some expert said. I let God speak to them through His Word under the direction of the Holy Spirit. And He does.

BIBLE-STORYING ERRORS

The skeptics may ask, "Doesn't telling Bible stories water down the truth or bring in errors?" It is our responsibility to be sure not to add to or leave out the truth of the Scriptures. We tell it like it is. Bible stories are true and transparent, even exposing the sins and faults of the biblical characters. We stay true to the text although we don't memorize it word for word. We tell it as a story so both we and those who hear it can remember it. Then they, in turn, can tell it to others. After someone tells or dramatizes a Bible story, we ask the listeners, "Did he leave out anything? Did he add anything?" just to be sure they remember it accurately.

Gossip? Not!

Someone may protest, "But doesn't the message get changed or diluted — like what happens in the game of Gossip, in which you whisper something in the ear of the person beside you, and each person whispers it in the ear of the next person until everyone in the circle has heard it? The message changes drastically by the time the last person hears it."

That has been our experience with the Gossip game, but something quite different happens when you change one factor to align with the storytelling practice in primary oral cultures. David Payne, a Wycliffe translator, conducts this learning game when introducing storying. In his groups, the first person tells the story out loud to the person beside her so that the whole circle of people hears it. Then that person repeats it out loud to the next and so forth until all the people in the group have heard it over and over. What do you think happens? The members immediately correct any errors in what was told because they own the story and feel they must preserve it. We tell Bible stories in a community that helps each member stay true to the Bible.

In America, we are blessed with freedom to access printed Bibles in about 450 languages.[4] Listeners can look at the texts themselves; this is a self-correcting aspect to Bible storying that is healthy. However, it does not diminish the importance and responsibility of the small-group leader and those preparing the Bible story to tell it as accurately as possible.

— Mark

FORGETFULNESS

"But what about the things we forget?" someone may ask. We admit that our memories are not perfect. That is why we depend on the written or recorded-verbatim Bible text as our source when we have access to it. Where the Bible is not available in the heart language of the people, translators may already be working zealously to translate the Scriptures so they can set the truth in text where it won't fade or change with time. Unfortunately, out of 6,900 languages in the world, only 451 languages have a complete Bible. Only 1,185 have an adequate New Testament, and 2,252 have no translation at all. And among those language groups that have a written translation, approximately 70 percent of the people can't read it with understanding.[5]

For those people groups that do have a translation in their heart language, several organizations, including Faith Comes By Hearing, produce audio Bibles so that all people who speak that language can hear the complete words of Scripture.[6] This gives them access to written texts for accuracy. For those groups still waiting for more extensive translations, organizations such as OneStory and The Seed Company start by translating twenty-five to sixty-five stories from creation to Christ. Wycliffe and its family of organizations check them to be sure the key terms are translated correctly.

If you or I do forget a detail of a story when we tell it, we correct our mistake as soon as we realize it. Often this happen in the dialogue session, and the storyteller remembers something he or she left out. That very fact alone helps our hearers remember it—sometimes better than if we didn't make the mistake in the first place!

TELL IT BY HEART

"If you don't *memorize* the story, then how do you remember it so you can tell it without looking at your Bible?" another person asks. We remember Scripture as we remember anything. Visualization. Repetition. Storyboarding. Checking the text. We read the text many times. We master the story by telling it aloud to one or two people and having them check the text to see if we told it accurately. If nobody is around, then we can simply record ourselves telling the story and listen to the playback while we check our Bibles.[7]

One very intriguing phenomenon occurs among people who can read but prefer not to. When they hear a Bible story told and engage the truth in dialogue, they study their Bibles more. Before I told the story of Stephen's martyrdom speech (see Acts 7) at an International Orality Network conference, I asked people to close their Bibles and listen to it as an oral story. Dorothy Miller, executive director of The God's Story Project, told me later that because she didn't believe something I said was in the Bible, she had peeked at her Bible underneath the table. She said, "I was amazed that it was right there and I had never noticed it before."[8] As a result of experiencing the power of Bible storying, Dorothy and her group have developed a sixty-five story set to follow the *God's Story* DVD, and her team has translated those stories into many languages.

TELLING STORIES TO NONBELIEVERS

You may wonder what to do about modern relativism and cultures that teach there is no absolute truth. The answer is simple: *Just tell the stories.* Stories are not just illustrations to prove our points; they are vehicles of God's truth. Even though some people won't believe, the Word has power to both convince and convict.

We use Bible storying with amazing effectiveness with people of other religions. The stories usually slip under the radar of any real or imagined defenses because we are not directly confronting their beliefs or arguing with them. If they are willing to hear enough stories, there is often a cumulative effect until they can't deny the truth of God's Word.

Several Muslim men kept coming into a restaurant operated by a Christian man and his wife. The men would often swap stories, so the restaurant owner decided to tell some stories of God's power from the Bible. After a few meals and story-swapping times together, one of the men said, "These stories of yours are really good, but it seems that they are from a bigger story." The owner said, "That's right. Would you like to hear the Big Story?" When the men agreed, the owner started at Genesis and began week after week telling the stories chronologically through the Bible. After about six weeks, the men asked, "Does your wife know these stories too?" When he said that she did, the men arranged for their wives to come and hear the Big Story from her. Soon, four of the men and their wives accepted Christ and began evangelizing among their own networks of friends using the Big Story.

We are not discounting apologetics. However, arguments usually don't convince people as much as they remove obstacles to belief. If you keep telling the stories and allow the Holy Spirit to do His work, He convinces the listeners. After all, that's His job (see John 16:8-15). The whole process of storying followed by dialogue allows the Spirit to teach us the Word.

An issue of Southwestern Baptist Theological Seminary's *SouthwesternNews* focused on text-driven preaching. The feature article reported president Paige Patterson's speaking about preaching the text of Scripture. As you read this account, notice how he used the same principles we are sharing with you to get the point across that the Spirit brings the Bible to life. Apply his example to the stories in the Scripture as well as hidden application of preaching from texts.

In a spring 2006 chapel service, President Paige Patterson presented the "perfect expository sermon." It was just one example of Patterson's attempts to teach a new generation of preachers how the Word of God should be proclaimed.

The perfect sermon, Patterson said, is a dry sponge.

Lifting a large, dry sponge before his audience, Patterson said that, just as this sponge was hard at its core and soft on the surface, even so a perfect sermon is organized and built around firm truths. At the same time, it is tender toward its audience.

Patterson continued his illustration by scribbling on a blank writing tablet with a black marker. The tablet, he explained, is the typical church crowd, and the markings are the hurts, fears, and concerns that listeners harbor in their hearts. He tried to clean the board with his dry sponge — "the perfect expository sermon" — but without success.

Patterson's audience then watched him as he walked across the stage and as he dipped the dry sponge in a bucket of water. Lifting the sponge out of the bucket, he said, "When your sermon literally is full of the Spirit of the living God, like that sponge is full of the liquid in the bucket, then and only then are you ready to walk into the pulpit." Walking back to the tablet, he wiped it with the wet sponge, and the marks disappeared: "Look what happens when the Spirit of the living God is present."[9]

The supernatural power of God makes truth stick when we use His inerrant Word under the power of the Holy Spirit, who fulfills His role of revealing it to us. Instead of being seduced by non-Christian viewpoints, the people of God need to hear afresh the Word of God and communicate it to others by the power of the Spirit of God.

QUESTIONS FOR REFLECTION

1. How can you cooperate effectively with the Holy Spirit to tell God's inerrant Word?
2. How can God's truth be preserved when Bible stories are told?
3. How can hearing Bible stories remove obstacles to belief?
4. What is the role of the Holy Spirit in making disciples?

CHAPTER 9

HOOKED FOR LIFE

I collect globes from all over the world and have scores of them in various sizes and of different materials displayed around my home. One Christmas, my family gave me a globe puzzle made of hundreds of pieces. Fortunately, they had already put the puzzle together for me. My first question was, "How did you get all the pieces to stick together and stay in the shape of a globe?"

"Easy," my daughter laughed. "We glued them." That globe has been in my library for years, and it is still in the same spherical shape as when they gave it to me.

A bigger question is this: How do we make God's truth stick in people's hearts so it actually transforms their lives? Simple. The glue is *discipleship*. In the first half of this book we discovered the pieces of this puzzle and why oral strategies work for both oral learners and oral-preference learners (as well as literate learners!). We used the loops imagery to show how to get truth into our *heads* and remember it. Then we looked at how to internalize truth by using Bible-storying sessions so that we own the truth in our *hearts* on an emotional and spiritual level. Now we'll explore the rest of the question Marcus Vegh posed: "How do you make *disciples* of oral learners?" How do we hook our *hands* and feet into the application of God's truth?

In the second half of the book, I will share with you the other side of the Velcro analogy—the joy of intentional small-group discipleship using storying that results in unprecedented growth in spiritual maturity and in numbers. We will custom-fit all the hooks of Scripture to our mental, emotional, and sensory loops in order to make God's truth stick to disciples like Velcro even in a Teflon world. This simplified diagram of the course shows the strategy God has taught me to ensure His truth sticks.

Maximum Stickability

I ride a bicycle regularly for exercise. I discovered that if I don't wear special shoes, my feet slip off and the pedals whack me on the back of my legs. Cycling shoes have Velcro straps that hold my feet in the pedals. I have ridden more than 14,000 miles and made millions of pedal strokes. The good news is that the three straps on each shoe have never failed. They work as designed because I mash them into place for a customized fit each time I put them on.

If I only lightly tap the Velcro strap, I put myself at risk. If I use only a few touch points of the Velcro strap, it pulls apart when counter pressure is applied as I race or pump up a hill. Instead, I line up the straps that hold the hooks with the shoe straps where the loops are attached. By smoothing the straps down and applying pressure, each strap engages the fasteners. That's the only way the shoes with Velcro straps allow me to pedal properly.

— Mark

FIRST STEPS IN DISCIPLE MAKING

As I considered the spherical puzzle, my mind flashed back to my first semester in college, when I enjoyed college life more than I studied. As I began the second semester, God confronted me with the fact that I was also playing around in my Christian life. I protested that I did everything my church asked me to do, but God said I was not following Him obediently in every area of my life. I possessed Christ as my Savior, but my Lord did not fully possess me. He challenged me with these words: "If anyone would come after me, he must deny himself and take up his cross daily and follow me" (Luke 9:23). I knew that I was at a crossroads. I could choose to either become a true disciple or stay a mediocre Christian for the rest of my life. I debated with God for several agonizing nights before finally committing myself to follow Him as His disciple in everything.

Jesus showed me clearly that discipleship is all about my relationship with Him. Here's what I have come to believe that biblical discipleship looks like: Discipleship is developing a personal, obedient, life-long relationship with Jesus Christ in which He transforms your character into Christlikeness, changes your values into Kingdom values, and involves you in His mission in the home, the church, and the world.[1]

Not long after my commitment to *become* a true disciple, I felt the responsibility to *make* disciples. I went through the normal struggles of learning to share my faith. After the Lord taught me how to witness and rely on the Holy Spirit, I saw more than thirty persons pray to receive Christ in the next three months. I was overjoyed until a fellow student, who had been trained by The Navigators while in the military, asked me, "Where are they now?"

"I don't know," I said. "I committed them to God."

"No," he replied. "God committed them to *you*."

So I learned and applied everything I could to help new Christians become disciples of Jesus. About a year later, I became the pastor of a country church. Imagine my surprise when I discovered that about 80 to 90 percent of the members were still spiritual infants, even though they had been Christians for decades! I began to ask God, "How do I get them excited about following Christ again, and how do I help them grow as disciples?" Through trial and error I began to learn how to do that, but it wasn't easy.

After two years I left that church to enter the seminary, and in my second semester I started a church. I was committed to building a church like those in Acts. However, it was not long before I found myself weighted down with the programs of my denomination. But I was not content to just do church as usual and continued to try out new ways to engage God's people in following Him. Over the next eight years I learned how to make disciples in small groups; I also took the group members with me to disciple them one-on-one.

After my wife and I moved to Indonesia to become missionaries, I discipled the first four men who professed faith in Christ by meeting with them and taking them with me to minister. I'll never forget the night when one of the men said to the others, "You know, we can go to the villages and preach ourselves. We've got it!"

I shouted "Hallelujah!" because they had both the confidence and the competence to evangelize and make disciples.

From these and other experiences God showed me His framework for allowing all types of learners, from highly literate to oral preference, not just to survive but to thrive in their growth as fully devoted disciples of Jesus. Now I saw clearly the full picture of making truth stick through my personal experiences of making disciples and using Bible stories to do so.

Do you find yourself somewhere in my story? In the chapters ahead I'll unfold the rest of the discipleship story and my delight in discovering how to make disciples as Jesus did. Jesus' last command was to make disciples of all nations. How are you doing?

ON TARGET

Matt Emmons was one shot away from the Olympic gold medal. Up to that point, he had dominated the men's fifty-meter three-position rifle target event at the 2004 Summer Olympics in Athens. All he needed was a score of 7.2 to win—and Emmons's lowest score on his first nine shots in the competition was a 9.3.

He took his position, focused on the crosshairs in his viewfinder, carefully brought the rifle down and honed in on the dead center of the target, steadied himself, took a slight breath, let it out a bit and held it, and gently squeezed the trigger. As soon as the firing pin hit the primer, he knew he had hit the bull's-eye. He had won his second gold medal!

But something was not right; the target had not registered the shot. The judges huddled and discussed allowing Emmons to shoot again because of the apparent malfunction until someone noticed an extra shot on the target in the next lane. Emmons had hit the bull's-eye—of the wrong target! He had fired at the target in lane three while shooting in lane two. The score did not count! He dropped to eighth place, and his dreams for that gold medal were filed forever in the overstuffed folder labeled "If only . . ."

Can you imagine investing such an extraordinary amount of time, emotion, energy, and resources into trying to hit that bull's-eye . . . and you finally hit it—only to find out that you were aiming at the wrong target!?[2]

Are you aiming at the wrong target? Are you and your church making disciples?

A REVEALING STUDY

In 2007 one of the largest churches in America, Willow Creek Community Church in South Barrington, Illinois (a suburb of Chicago), published *Reveal,* a book reporting results from a three-year study. Willow Creek's leaders discovered that they were failing to disciple a significant number of their church members. It wasn't that they weren't making disciples at all, but nearly one out of four of their most mature believers was stalled in his or her spiritual growth or dissatisfied with the church—and many people were considering leaving.[3]

The study sent shock waves through many churches that followed the Willow Creek "seeker church" model. Willow Creek's leadership went into the survey assuming that there was a positive correlation between involvement in church activity and spiritual growth. After they got the results, the church offered numerous courses that its members could take and activities they could be involved in. To Pastor Bill Hybels and his church leaders' credit, they not only owned up to the problem and took steps to change but also exposed their errors by publishing a book so others could learn from their mistakes.

HOW IS BUSINESS?

Since we know the Great Commission, we should know what our business is: making disciples. Jesus said to His disciples,

I no longer call you servants, because a servant does not know his master's business. Instead, I have called you friends, for everything that I learned from my Father I have made known to you. . . . I chose you and appointed you to go and bear fruit—fruit that will last. (John 15:15-16)

The Father's business and ours is to *make disciples that last* (see also Matthew 28:18-20).

How are you and your church doing with the business He has entrusted to you? Let's examine the expectations of a business. If a factory produces widgets, its manager asks three questions:

- "How many widgets did we produce?"
- "What quality were our widgets?"
- "What is our market penetration?"

The word *disciple* means "learner" as well as "follower." Universities ask the same questions:

- "How many students did we have?"
- "What quality are our graduates?"
- "What impact are our graduates making in the world?"

Businesses and universities work diligently to achieve their goals, and they measure their results.

How well would you and your ministry fare if asked to evaluate how you are doing in the Master's business of making disciples? You can ask those same questions:

- How *is* business?
- How many disciples did your church make last year?
- What quality of disciples did you produce?
- What was your penetration into the world with those disciples?

THE GLUE OF DISCIPLESHIP

Obedience and accountability are two major bonding elements in discipleship. How much time and effort does your present small group or Bible-study class take to make specific applications and ensure that members put them into practice individually and as a group? The TruthSticks strategy leads people to obey the commands and examples in the stories. Obedience is simple to talk about but not so easy to do. Margie Blanchard, wife of author Ken Blanchard (*The One Minute Manager, Lead Like Jesus*), said, "The gap between knowing and doing is significantly greater than the gap between ignorance and knowledge."[4]

It is funny how those of us familiar with the content of the Bible can overlook the obvious. I saw I was not getting through to one audience as I spoke about obedience, so I invited them to stand and sing the children's song "The Wise Man Built His House Upon the Rock." I even led them in the hand motions.

After we finished, people laughed as they sat down. I told them I had gone through that exercise to emphasize a point about Jesus' story that I wanted them never to forget. Then I asked them, "What is the rock?"

The answers came quickly in succession, "Jesus," "the Bible," and "the church."

"No," I said after each answer. "You see those answers in other places in the Bible, but not in this story by Jesus."

After ten or twelve other answers, someone shouted, "Obedience!" I agreed and pointed out what Jesus said in His story: "Everyone who hears these words of mine and *puts them into practice* is like a wise man who built his house on the rock. . . . But everyone who hears these words of mine and does *not* put them into practice is like a foolish man who built his house on sand" (Matthew 7:24,26, emphasis added). Both men heard the words of Jesus, but only one obeyed. This was Jesus' closing point to the Sermon on the Mount that many of us nod agreement to but don't put into practice. Just before He told the above story about obedience, Jesus said, "Why do you call me, 'Lord, Lord,' and do not do what I say?" (Luke 6:46).

Then I quoted this verse: "Whoever has my commands and obeys them, he is the one who loves me. He who loves me will be loved by my Father, and I too will love him and show myself to him" (John 14:21). I said, "Those of you who love Jesus, hold up your hand." After they did I responded, "That's *almost* unanimous. Now let me ask you, how many of you obey Christ's commands?" Four or five hands shot up, and a number of other people put their hands up halfway. Others were unsure. I asked, "What's wrong? That is the same question. Jesus said that if you love Him, you will obey His commands."

I admitted that we all have a problem with that question because we realize that we fall far short of perfect obedience. But those are Jesus' words, and He ties our obedience to our love relationship with Him. The key words in this definition of *discipleship* are *personal, obedient relationship with Christ*. The word *obedient* is in the middle of *personal relationship with Christ* and glues the two together. Obedience means that we love the Lord our God with all our hearts, all our souls, and all our minds and that we do what He says. Obedience sticks truth to life.

Obedience to God's truth is the measure of success in discipleship. This establishes the Bible as the authority rather than the group's leader, protecting the group against personality cults or theological deviations creeping in. Obedience to Christ's commands results in tremendous fruitfulness (see John 15:5). It proves God's truth has *stuck*.

Telling all the stories in the Bible will not make disciples; you must be intentional about making disciples. The more people participate in the dialogue, tell stories themselves, help the group process the story, and hold each other accountable to obeying the truth, the more they get the stories into their lives and obey the truths in them. If they passively receive the Bible without truly engaging God's truth, they will not apply it. They will never take the initiative to share their faith and make disciples.

ACCOUNTABILITY THROUGH
SUPPORTIVE RELATIONSHIPS

Accountability takes place in a supportive group. It amazes me to
see how quickly people respond to Bible stories in the right kind of
relational groups and how easily they apply them. Lisa Sells (editor
for Jim Putman's book *Real-Life Discipleship*) attended the Immersion
I training at Real Life Ministries. This two-day event is offered for
staff members from other churches who want to learn about Real Life
Ministries' process of making disciples.

Lisa told me,

> I had read some of the material about orality and storying, so
> I intellectually knew what it was. Then I went to Immersion I;
> we were in a small group, and we had this guy from the church
> who introduced himself as being retired from the military.
> He had been in the Marines for twenty years. He stood up
> and started telling the story of the prodigal son. You could
> tell he had practiced it. No embellishment, just standing there
> quietly telling the story. And everyone in the group of thirteen
> was caught up in his telling that story. When it was over, he
> asked very simple questions related to the story: "Which one
> of the people in this story do you most relate to: the father, the
> prodigal son, or the older brother?"
>
> It was like the floodgates were opened. One guy said he
> was like the father because his kid was struggling. Another
> said he related to the prodigal son because "That was me!"
> The first person was so honest and transparent about what was
> going on in his life that it went around the circle like we were
> family. I said to myself, *Oh my gosh—this works!* It was just
> someone opening up a story and letting us get into it where
> we are in our lives and where we are intersecting with that

story. What that guy had done—there was nothing fancy about it, anyone could have done it—made me realize that Bible storying worked by letting everyday people spread the message. That's when I became a believer. It was not someone explaining anything to us; he was just opening the Bible up to us.[5]

Ask yourself, How well is my church or ministry doing at getting our members to apply the truth in the midst of real-life experiences? Are the disciples making good choices? Do they demonstrate an appreciation for God's Word in their everyday lives? Can they communicate God's truths to others in their own words without being prompted or nagged? What do their calendars and checking accounts reveal about their priorities? When problems hit, can they troubleshoot by relying on stories they have embedded in their hearts? Are they openly communicating God's truth with those they encounter at home, at school, shopping, working, working out, or at play?

In other words, are they obedient disciples, participating in a supportive group relationship and experiencing spiritual transformation in Christ?

HOOKED FOR LIFE

The key to getting truth to stick practically and permanently is to help people obey the truth in a participative, supportive, and accountability-building group. The next subtle but indispensable element in making God's truth stick in life, for life, is the leader setting the right example by intentionally making disciples. We will look at that model in the next chapter.

QUESTIONS FOR REFLECTION

1. How personal and obedient is your relationship with Christ?
2. Is your character being transformed into Christ's likeness on a regular basis?
3. Which kingdom values are not yet your core values?
4. How effective is your church or ministry in making disciples? Are you making disciples of others? If not, why not start with two or three right away?
5. How are you involved in God's mission at home, in your church, and around the world?

CHAPTER 10

JESUS' WAY OF MAKING TRUTH STICK

Ken Sorrells, a missionary friend, told me the story of Elias Cuc Quim. Elias was one of the first pastors in the Kekchi work in Guatemala and was greatly admired for his wisdom, Bible knowledge, and faithfulness to the Lord. Although severe diabetes kept him homebound for many years, he made a remarkable recovery. Ken noticed Elias, now able to walk again, frequently walking and talking with several younger men behind him. They would walk for a while and then stop. Walk some more and stop. Each time they stopped, Elias would be speaking very intently. It was evident these walks were more than casual strolls.

To ease his curiosity, Ken caught up with Elias and his small group and asked him what they were doing. Elias replied, "I'm teaching my disciples." When asked to explain, Elias said, "I saw the *JESUS* film not long ago, and I saw that Jesus spent much of His time walking and teaching His disciples. Because I believe we should follow the example of our Lord, I began to teach these young men about the Bible and church work the same way Jesus taught the men who would continue on after He was gone." The young men would then return to their villages and repeat the process, discipling "just the way Jesus did."[1]

How do you make disciples in the twenty-first century as Jesus and the disciples did in the first century? Wouldn't it be easier to make disciples as Jesus did if the people you were discipling were with you twenty-four hours a day, seven days a week? Or if you lived in an easygoing oral society as Elias did? But in the twenty-first century? We can't spend every day with disciples for three years in our fast-paced era of globalization. Forget it.

On the other hand, that was Jesus' final command. Did He give the Great Commission only to the Twelve? If that were true, it would have died when they died. No, He gave it to all of His followers, and we see it lived out in the rest of the New Testament. So after the Holy Spirit confronted me with the Great Commission, I began to obey Jesus' command.

BEGIN AT THE END

As I explored the stories of Jesus choosing His disciples, the Lord showed me that if I wanted to make disciples as Jesus did, I should begin with the end in mind. Jesus knew the purpose of the Father for the disciples before He began His ministry with them. He spent all night in prayer before He chose His disciples. We only understand His end vision by listening to Him pray the night before He was crucified. Jesus prayed to the Father for His disciples: "I have brought you glory on earth by completing the work you gave me to do" (John 17:4).

What had He completed? He tells us in His prayer: "I have revealed you to those whom you gave me out of the world. They were yours; you gave them to me and they have obeyed your word. Now they know that everything you have given me comes from you. . . . As you sent me into the world, I have sent them into the world" (John 17:6-7,18).

Jesus completed the work of discipling the Twelve by giving them the words from the Father, helping them obey, and sending them into the world to do the work of the Father. His disciple making was not accidental; it was *intentional*. Jesus said, "A student is not above his teacher, but everyone who is fully trained will be like his teacher" (Luke 6:40). Jesus intends for us to make disciples as He did. It was His work, and now it is our work. If we follow His example, we will intentionally make disciples as He did.

VISIBLE MODELS

After John baptized Jesus, he said, "Look, the Lamb of God!" and two of John's disciples followed Jesus. Jesus showed a personal interest in them and asked, "What do you want?" When they asked where He was staying, He invited them to come and spend time with Him. Two other disciples started following Jesus that same day, and then others soon joined them. In the next three years Jesus progressively spent more and more of His time with the disciples preparing them for the work He was going to do through them.

Consider for a moment what it must have been like to follow Jesus every day. The Twelve traveled on a regular basis as Jesus led. They were amazed by the miracles they saw. Jesus' teachings were fresh and authoritative, communicated in the context of the world they knew. Jesus' disciples were never allowed to get into a routine of repetition. Yet they were on a progressive path of unprecedented spiritual growth. That three-year crucible of time was enough to launch a global movement that will continue until Jesus returns.

When the disciples faced difficult situations after Jesus returned to the Father, they could easily recall what He had done in hundreds of real-life situations and apply His example. When the visitors to Jerusalem were hungry after Pentecost, the disciples fed them. When Peter and John met the crippled man, they healed him. When the disciples were persecuted, they praised God and prayed for their persecutors. They followed His example.

After I reached the conclusion that I was to make disciples, I said, "But no one has personally discipled me. How do I know how to disciple anyone else?" My parents had helped me develop as a Christian as I was growing up, but I did not know how to disciple adults. But, I reasoned, since Jesus chose His disciples as adults, He could be my model, and the Holy Spirit would disciple me to become like Christ. Since I did not find just one person to disciple me, I sought out many people as models and tried to emulate the Christlike characteristics in each one. I was also inspired by and learned much from the biographies of Christian leaders.

However, I still felt I needed a person who was following Christ to help me follow Him. I began to look for someone to disciple me. After I started the church in Fort Worth, I visited a weekly Bible study of The Navigators in Dallas and saw the people there modeling what I wanted to be. I kept asking leaders there to disciple me but was discouraged when they told me to just keep coming to Bible study. After hounding the director, Skip Gray, until he was convinced I meant business, he began driving to Fort Worth every week to train me in the basic how-tos of discipleship. I thought, *I would drive to Dallas to speak to a crowd, but would I drive that far every week to meet with one person?* He taught me by example that we must show personal attention and give individual help to people to disciple them. After Skip was transferred three months later, I sought out other disciplers, and they collectively helped me understand many things Jesus did to make disciples of His followers.

GETTING INVOLVED

Jesus got involved in His disciples' lives to get them involved in His life. He went to Peter's house and healed his mother-in-law. He got in Peter's boat and asked him to push it out into the water so He could teach the crowd. He got involved in Peter's business when He told him to cast in the deeper water and catch more fish than he could haul in. He got the disciples involved in His work when He said, "Don't be afraid; from now on you will catch men" (Luke 5:10).

I learned to take a personal interest in the lives of those I discipled. I got involved in their everyday lives. I got them involved in serving with me by deciding that I would not do anything by myself when I could take someone else with me. If I made a hospital visit, went to witness to a non-Christian, or dealt with a problem that was not confidential, I would take one of the men I was discipling with me. They saw me live out the truth in real-life situations before I asked them to do it. Step by step, I taught them to do what I was doing, but I was constantly aware that I had to model it before I taught it. Rather than their presence being a hindrance, I was multiplying my ministry by discipling men as I served others.

I took one of my group members with me to witness with the intent of training him as a witness. The first time we went together, all I asked him to do was watch what I did and pray. He said afterward, "You don't expect me to be able to do what you did, do you?" Then he added, "Well, I guess you do, because you do it."

Jesus is the best example of how we should make disciples. His invitation was to first "Follow *Me*" (author's emphasis) instead of to believe a certain theology, live up to a specific code of conduct, or become a member of a particular group. His call was distinctively personal. We are not making personal disciples, but helping them become disciples of Jesus and follow Him.

First the disciples bonded with Jesus. He demonstrated how they were to follow His example by showing them that He was following the example of His Father, and He told them so: "I tell you the truth, the Son can do nothing by himself; he can do only what he sees his Father doing, because whatever the Father does the Son also does" (John 5:19). Jesus was not just telling stories; He *was* God's story in real life, and the disciples could "read" Him every day and night. But telling stories was one way Jesus made disciples.

Because we are imperfect examples, it is crucial for us to be honest about our shortcomings. Brandon Guindon (in The Moose Call on page 84) modeled the proper response when he called two of the guys in his small group to help find the new convert, Mike, and pack out his moose. But the rest of the story is that as Brandon recounted the experience to his pastors' seminar the next morning, and later to Mike, he admitted his feelings: "I was disgruntled and grumpy. I kept asking, 'What are You doing, Lord? I have to teach in the morning.'" He could have left out that part of the story, but when he admitted his emotions, people knew he was real and could identify with him.

Although we can't spend twenty-four hours a day, seven days a week with disciples in the twenty-first century, there are several things we can do to replicate the close relationship. We can develop a transparent small group and become friends so that we do other things together and help one another. Some of the greatest spiritual lessons are learned at play. We develop close relationships by meeting individuals for breakfast, serving others together, or by leading a smaller group of men or women. We can bridge our relationships as needed with telephone calls, e-mails, Twitter, Facebook, and other media so we have many interactions in real life. When we live out Christ's model in daily life, people get it. When the Word, the Spirit, and our model align, people have a deep longing to be like Jesus.

EXPLAINING

A model does not stand alone; it often needs explanation. At times Jesus explained after He modeled something (see Matthew 17:20; Mark 9:29). After Jesus washed the disciples' feet, He explained, "Now that I, your Lord and Teacher, have washed your feet, you also should wash one another's feet. I have set you an example that you should do as I have done for you" (John 13:14-15).

At other times Jesus would teach something to the crowds and then explain it to the disciples in private (see Mark 4:10-20; 7:17-23). Sometimes Jesus explained what He was going to do before He did it (see Mark 10:32-34). He explained His death to the disciples beforehand so they would understand what was happening when the Jewish rulers killed Him (see Matthew 16:21). Explanation etches the model in our memories.

After I told the first Bible story in one small group, I asked for a volunteer to tell a new story at the next session. Jason volunteered, and we met after the group time to go over how he would tell the story. I explained in simple terms what I had done and why I had done it. I asked him if he had any questions. I asked him to repeat my explanation of how I told the story and led the dialogue. I made sure he knew the model and understood how to do it. I asked him to practice the story on his own and then be ready to tell it to me before he told the story to the group.

COACHING

Jesus developed His disciples by coaching them. Coaching carries with it the intimate picture of a discipler guiding a disciple to do something more effectively and skillfully until the disciple becomes comfortable with the new way of doing things. Coaching includes telling someone what *not* to do as well as what *to* do. A wise coach knows when to let people learn on their own and when to intervene.

In my earlier example, I asked Jason to meet with me before the rest of the group gathered to tell the story again before he told the group. I then coached him on how to tell it better. He did an excellent job of telling the story and leading the dialogue in the group session. Afterward we debriefed what happened, and I praised him and gave him coaching tips so he could do even better the next time. I coached him so he could be successful the first time he told a story.

Jesus developed His disciples by commanding them to put His teachings into practice right away. There was never a graduation day. They did what He told them on their own, but Jesus was always nearby to coach them and talk afterward.

Coaching for Life

As a former wrestling coach, Jim Putman, pastor of Real Life Ministries, uses the coaching analogy for discipling. He said, "A coach has to know the game from personal experience. Leaders cannot lead from inexperience. You must know the gospel, what the battle for men's souls is, and what kind of attacks to expect so you are not easily discouraged.

"Second, a coach has to know his players and where they are in their development. Good coaching requires the leader to watch and evaluate his players accurately so that they can be positioned to win. This requires him to spend time with his players.

"Third, the coach has to get them on the playing field. Ministry is the playing field. Disciples cannot reach their God-given potential without a safe place to 'play' and learn the game of disciple making. Once the coach knows where they are, he knows what he must do to help each player be the best he can be. The small-group environment using Bible storying is the best place to learn. It gives disciples a chance to 'play' in a nonthreatening environment so they can grow and the coach can discern their maturity."[2]

— Jim Putman

Support

The disciples put the things Jesus taught them into practice right away because the lessons were a part of the life they encountered *together* (apprenticeship). Once people have learned a truth, skill, or lifestyle, they still need support to help them practice it. The disciples knew that their Master would support them in whatever He told them to do. When apprentices learn what they can from a master, they are ready to launch out on their own. As growing apprentices begin to live their new lifestyles and do their new work, they are assured that someone more experienced is backing them up, ready to counsel them, give them feedback, and help them continue to develop.

Empowering

Most of us need someone or some group to validate our ministries. Jesus did that when He told Peter, "Feed my sheep" (John 21:17), and, "Strengthen your brothers" (Luke 22:32). Jesus finished His work of training the disciples to lead by commissioning and empowering them to "make disciples of all nations" (see Matthew 28:18-20; Acts 1:8). Jesus set the pattern for a formula we use in discipleship: Model, Assist, Watch, and Leave! Yes, leave as Jesus did and let them lead the process with others.

I enjoyed playing tag when I was a kid. At some point, another kid would tap me on the shoulder and yell for everyone to hear, "Tag! You're it!" Adrenaline would shoot through my body, and I'd run as fast as I could to tag one of my buddies, making them "it." When you're it, you have had authority bestowed upon you to fulfill a purpose you are fully capable of doing on your own. The Holy Spirit provides the power to fulfill the call to make disciples as Jesus did.

One of the reasons Christians do not perform the ministries God has given them is they do not feel that they have the authority to do them. Tag 'em! Release those who display desired leadership skills and heart. The new leaders in your midst who are bearing fruit for the kingdom and have the right attitudes and behaviors must be empowered and released to start their own groups, whether in your church or among other people where a new church is needed.

Jim Blazin, home-groups pastor of Real Life Ministries, said, "Our home groups are growing. We have probably added sixty-five to seventy groups this season, which is decent growth. Could we do more? Absolutely! But discipleship takes time. We have to be patient with the growth process and allow the things that we are walking our people through to catch up and actually impact them."[3]

When our overarching purpose is to intentionally make disciples, we start with modeling how others are to live. We invite others to walk with us. We explain as necessary until they understand. We also coach along the way and support them in their efforts. Our relationships reinforce the Scripture lessons they encounter to the point that they are empowered to launch out on their own to continue making even more disciples as Jesus did. Discipling as Jesus did makes God's truth stick.

QUESTIONS FOR REFLECTION

1. How could you be more intentional in making disciples?
2. What is your end vision for believers whom God leads you to disciple?
3. As an intentional leader, how can you get more involved in the lives of those you are discipling?
4. What are ways that you have seen godly leaders train, coach, or support someone they were mentoring?
5. How can you empower those you are discipling to step out on their own?

CHAPTER II

THE SPIRITUAL-GROWTH STORY

The first time some people hear about using Bible stories to make God's truth stick in their lives, their initial reaction is, "Bible stories are for children." Of course they are, but everyone loves a story. Adults spend much of their leisure time telling stories, reading novels, and going to movies. In fact, the older we get, the more we love stories! God has created us to love stories so much that the same story from the Bible can be used at any stage of spiritual growth and still apply to everyone in a group. I learned early in my ministry that people remembered my stories far better than my preaching points. I just didn't know how to tell the Bible stories as the content and get my listeners involved in interpreting and applying them, rather than using stories as illustrations of theological points.

In the previous chapter we looked at spiritual growth from the perspective of the intentional leader who plans to develop disciples to be like Jesus in character and conduct. This chapter explores the developmental process that we grow through as disciples and how we can help people mature through using Bible stories.

Each Christian has a *spiritual-growth story* that spans from new birth to maturity. Your personal spiritual-growth story tells your progress in the Christian life and how well you align with God's story. As we grow in Christlikeness, it is a story worth telling!

DEVELOPING A SPIRITUAL-GROWTH STORY

When I was president of the Indonesian Baptist Theological Seminary, the staff and I realized that most of the seminary students had not been adequately discipled. Because the seminary curriculum assumed they had been discipled in their churches, we were giving them the second and third levels of theological education without a strong foundation of discipleship. We identified several stages of spiritual growth: from the "dead" person who has not believed, to the new Christian who becomes a spiritual child, a spiritual disciple, a disciple maker, and a leader of the whole process.[1]

I took the seminary staff and some of the trustees to a mountain retreat for several days to see if we could describe the characteristics of each level of spiritual growth from the Bible and identify how to help students develop through each successive stage. We developed a curriculum that addressed all the stages, both the ones the students needed themselves and the ones they would lead their church members to experience.

At that retreat, we also discussed the foundational concept that fathers have children. They reproduce. Good fathers love their children and are concerned about passing on skills and knowledge to them at every stage of growth. These fathers want to become grandfathers who are able to lead their descendants through the whole process because of their experience. In the spiritual realm, *they want a reproducible process of spiritual growth that will help disciples make disciples who make disciples!*

In fact, I was so convicted about my personal disciple making after our retreat that I chose someone in each stage to disciple and to help me learn the needs of each stage of growth. I witnessed to Sudriano, a worker on the seminary grounds, and led him to Christ; then I began to teach him to walk in his new faith. I was already discipling Santoso, the manager of the seminary facilities, who needed to learn the basics of the Christian life because he still acted like a spiritual child. At the same time, I began to disciple my pastor, Markus, to mature in his faith as a spiritual disciple. I was discipling Sudiono, the academic dean, to be a disciple maker. I mentored Marvin, a seminary professor, as we worked together to develop discipleship-training materials to assist disciples at each level. These experiences helped me learn how to disciple persons at every stage of growth. I have not always found it strategic to be simultaneously discipling persons at every level, but this was very helpful to me to understand the full process.

Out of those experiences we developed the principles and processes that I wrote about in *MasterLife,* a curriculum that has been translated into fifty-two languages and has helped hundreds of thousands of people become reproducing disciples. And those same biblical principles in *MasterLife* are embedded in the *Following Jesus* audio series, my consultation with Real Life Ministries in Idaho, and the TruthSticks approach spelled out in this book.

TRACKING SPIRITUAL GROWTH

The *Following Jesus* storying group used the *MasterLife* process to choose stories to make disciples at every stage of the Christian life. My involvement with Real Life Ministries gave me a good place in the United States to test the storying-based model of discipleship that worked so well overseas. Real Life Ministries' executive staff, community pastors, and small-group leaders made it easy, because they were already focused on making disciples of all the people in their church. As we discussed this model of spiritual progression, the team came up with the following diagram to show normal development as it applied to discipleship.

Reading clockwise from the top, you see the following stages: dead (in sins), infant, child, young adult, and parent.

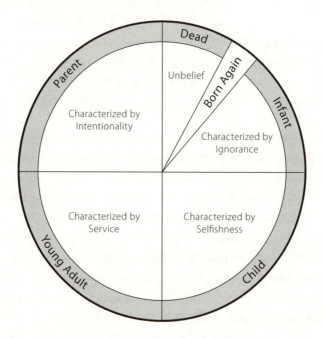

One of the remarkable things about storying in a group is that people at all the stages of development can grow at their own pace, much like children grow in a family.

Dead: The Non-Christian: Characterized by Unbelief

From an evangelical point of view, 90 percent of the world's population doesn't claim to have a personal relationship with Christ. Another 20 percent calls themselves Christians but would not be considered evangelicals or born again.[2] We all start out as unbelievers and fit Paul's description: "As for you, you were dead in your transgressions and sins" (Ephesians 2:1).

The task at this stage is for the intentional discipleship leader and the group members to share the gospel with the unbeliever. The beautiful thing about storying to unbelievers is that it gives them an interesting, easy way to grasp the story of the gospel. When storying occurs in a relational group with an intentional leader, unbelievers have a place conducive to discovering God's plan for their lives.

At Home in the Family

Luke Yetter was raised in the woods of northern Idaho by his mother, a New Age guru. When Luke got out on his own, he discovered he had a capacity to make money in business and became a multimillionaire. After he got married, he wanted to avoid divorce and the kind of upbringing he had experienced. Luke reasoned that Christians had more stable marriages, so he and his wife visited several churches but did not understand what was going on and felt they weren't very friendly. When he visited Real Life Ministries, the people were friendly and what they said rang true to life.

Luke and his wife were invited to a home group. The first night they attended, the story was about the three Hebrew captives who were thrown into the fiery furnace (see Daniel 3). He connected with the story because of the contrast between his mother's New Age practices and the young Hebrews' commitment not to bow to other gods. As the session came to a close, Luke blurted out, "I need to get something straight. I don't understand this story about Shadrach,

My-Shack, and To-Bed-We-Go." After a big laugh, the group members surrounded him, explained the names of the men, and helped him understand the story. That began a relationship that resulted in Luke and his wife following Jesus. Their spiritual growth was so rapid that in a few years Luke was asked to lead the Real Life Association, which helps other churches learn how to become disciple-making churches.[3]

— Avery

Infant Believers: Characterized by Ignorance

In 1 Peter 2:2-3 we read: "Like newborn babies, crave pure spiritual milk, so that by it you may grow up in your salvation, now that you have tasted that the Lord is good." It is the job of the parent to be sure that the newborn baby has milk; it is the task of the leader and the group to build relationships with new believers and connect them to God's truth. New Christians in the infant stage need to be *connected* to a small group that will help them be *connected* to Christ on a regular basis through all the means available.

Children: Characterized by Selfishness

For ease in understanding how to minister to the people in this stage, Real Life Ministries distinguishes between the *infant* (a new believer) and the *child* (a person who became a Christian years ago but has not grown). Those in the child stage are still "me-centered." They are apathetic toward the Christian life.

In cases where people have not grown after coming to Christ, they are characterized as children because they still act like spiritual infants. Paul said, "Brothers, I could not address you as spiritual but as worldly—mere infants in Christ. I gave you milk, not solid food, for you were not yet ready for it. Indeed, you are still not ready. You are still worldly" (1 Corinthians 3:1-3; see also Hebrews 5:11-12).

Although their growth has been dormant for years, people at this child stage can be led to grow. Ashley Hall attends Trinity Point Baptist Church in Easley, South Carolina, where they use Bible storying in small groups. She feels deeply the importance of helping believers navigate through the whole maturation process. She told about one man who started out as self-centered but began to grow:

> We've got a guy in our small group. He was what we would consider a spiritual child—not very involved at all. One time his wife had to work, but he came in to our church service and sat with our small group—a huge accomplishment. And then recently he met this guy in his neighborhood and invited him to our small group. He was the first person in our whole small group to invite someone and have them come on in. We just thought that was awesome to come to church, invite someone, and he's actually led a session all by himself. We've seen a lot of spiritual growth.[4]

Young Adults: Characterized by Service

The apostle John wrote to the young men "because you are strong, and the word of God lives in you, and you have overcome the evil one" (1 John 2:14). Spiritual young adults are becoming "others-centered" and look out for others' needs.

Ashley's husband, Chad, said,

> There's a guy in our group who was a car salesman. Selling cars with this economy was not going well, so he gathered all of his sales staff together. With the owners on the speakerphone, he began to tell the entire story of Joseph to them! He didn't know if he was going to lose his job or not for doing it. Afterward, the owners said, "This is the best sales meeting we ever had. Yeah, times are tough, but there's a God who's bigger

than our bad times." And he was just walking them through the story he had heard.[5]

Spiritual young adults choose to minister to others. Whether that service is working with others in the church or helping with a ministry for outsiders, they are no longer looking out for just themselves.

Parents: Characterized by Intentionality

A person in this stage watches others develop in ministry and intentionally disciples them to multiply and become reproducers themselves. The emphasis at this stage is reproduction. When disciples are parents, they are not only concerned about the growth of their own family (small group) but the vitality of those around them (church) and those they must intentionally reach out to reproduce among (evangelism and missions). In chapter 15 we will examine ways that disciples not only reproduce themselves but also see their "offspring" begin to multiply.

REAL-LIFE EXPERIENCE

The second part of developing a spiritual-growth story for believers is for the group leader to recognize the level of maturity of the people in the group and take appropriate steps to help them grow. The more the members grow, the more leaders must give them an opportunity "to play in the game." The process the leader uses to help people move from one stage to the next at Real Life Ministries is built around these concepts: Share, Connect, Minister, and Disciple (SCMD).

As you can see, this diagram is expanded from the diagram on page 138 and details the levels of spiritual growth and what we are to do at each stage.

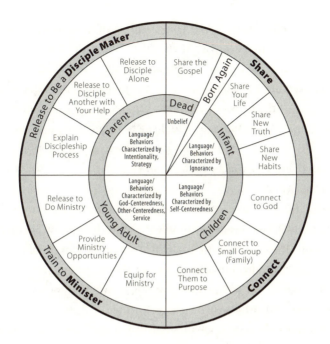

JESUS' INTENTIONAL DISCIPLESHIP PROCESS

JESUS	THE EARLY CHURCH
Share: Matthew 4:19; Luke 5:1-4	**Share:** Acts 2:1-39
Connect: Mark 9:30-31; John 3:22	**Connect:** Acts 2:40–4:37
Minister: Luke 9:1-6	**Minister:** Acts 6
Disciple: Matthew 28	**Disciple:** Acts 8

SHARE, CONNECT, MINISTER, DISCIPLE[6]

Jim Putman, Jim Blazin, and probably any small-group leader at Real Life Ministries can describe SCDM as a biblical process that Jesus used. He would *share* who He was with people, and they would respond.

Then He would *connect* with them and develop a relationship. He would teach them, walk with them, hang out with them, and model for them. When they grew and began to serve, He would move them into the *minister* phase. In the ministry phase He would send them out by twos — the twelve and the seventy-two — to serve, and then He would debrief them afterward. Finally, when they were ready to *disciple* others, He commissioned them. He gave them a place to practice, He watched them and coached them, and finally He sent them out to reproduce the process.

Real Life Ministries' staff members teach their small-group leaders to listen for specific kinds of comments from their group members to help them identify which stage the people are in and how to use the SCMD process to help them.

They call it "the phrase from the stage" (sometimes referred to as "the phrase from the phase").[7]

Spiritually dead people will say things like "I don't know that the Bible is true" or "I think that I will get to heaven because I am as good as the next person." As disciplers, we *share* the gospel with them in appropriate ways to bring them to Christ.

At the infant stage, when believers are new to the faith, the discipler will hear statements like "What am I supposed to do now?" or "How do you pray?" Our task as a discipler of those in the infant stage is to *share* our lives with them, *share* new truth that challenges them, and *share* new habits to help them progress in their spiritual lives.

In the spiritual child stage, the person might say, "I'm too busy to read my Bible," or, "I have been in the church all my life and I have never heard about that." The discipler hears a lot of *I* and *me* in the person's conversations. Once people in the child stage get connected to the group, their self-centeredness manifests itself in new ways. They begin to say things like "I love my group" and "Don't you ever branch my group." Sometimes they even do some ministry, but it is more for what they can get out of it than the help they can give the person in need. At this point, the discipler *connects* the people to God, *connects* them to the small group, and *connects* them to God's purpose.

When group members start to grow to the young-adult stage, the leader listens for their language to change to others-centered conversations. They will say things like "We need to reach out to Joe because he is having a hard time" or "Susan is sick; we need to watch her kids and take them some food." At this point, the discipler equips them to *minister*, gives them opportunities to *minister*, and then releases them to do their own *ministry*.

The discipler will hear people in the parent stage say, "I need to raise up someone to help in this ministry," or, "Did you notice how that person is growing in ministry? I think he or she can be discipled to lead that ministry." At that point, the discipler needs to explain the discipleship process to the disciples, help them as they *disciple* another person, and then release them to *disciple* someone on their own.

A REPRODUCIBLE PROCESS

When I first started consulting with Real Life Ministries, Jim Putman and his executive team asked me the question "Can storying also take believers to the next level into discipleship and leadership?" Now Jim is one of the strongest proponents.

> Here is where orality is so important. By creating an atmosphere where stories are being told and questions are being asked, you know where people are by what they say. You know what you need to do to help them grow to the next stage. If you know the *Share, Connect, Minister, Disciple* process and the "phrase from the phase," you know where they are by their comments, and you can help them. When you use questions, people open up, and you can know what they know about God, what they understand, and what they are doing with the information.[8]

Jim Putman and the Real Life Ministry home groups do not limit discipling to what takes place within the home groups. Most of the male leaders also have meetings with the men, and women lead women's groups separately at other times to go more in-depth with issues that are easier to address in gender-specific groups. The small-group leaders and members also work with individuals one-on-one to help them move to the next stage in the spiritual-growth story.

All of us have a spiritual-growth story. The more we align with God's story, the more we grow in His likeness. We all need a leader and a group to help us experience maximum growth. We all should be helping others in the stages we have passed through. In the next chapter we will discuss how to choose stories for discipling based on the worldview of the people you are serving and how to help them deal with barriers, bridges, and gaps in their lives.

QUESTIONS FOR REFLECTION

1. Jot down the highlights of your own spiritual-growth story.
2. Using the diagram on page 143, which stage best describes you?
3. How are you helping people in the stages you have already grown through? How can you disciple them with what you know from your present stage of growth?
4. How does using Bible storying assist in helping disciples mature to the point of being leaders?
5. How can you be a leader and a follower simultaneously?

CHAPTER 12

A NEW OPERATING SYSTEM FOR WORLDVIEW

Remember the heartrending story of Matt Emmons losing the gold medal at the 2004 Olympics in the men's rifle event because he hit the bull's-eye of the target, but in the wrong lane? He got his chance for redemption at the 2008 Olympics in Beijing. Emmons averaged 10.1 points on his first nine shots in the final round. He needed only a score of 7.0 to earn the top spot on the podium. This time, as he carefully lowered his rifle downward to focus on the bull's-eye, he accidentally hit the trigger and set off a shot that hit seven rings wide of the target's center. His misfire gave the gold medal to Qui Jian of China.[1] No one could believe that it had happened again!

It's possible to hit the target of disciple making and still miss the bull's-eye. The bull's-eye is the worldview of the people we are trying to disciple. I am going to ask you to look at a scary diagnosis of the worldview of young Americans; this is necessary to find a prescription for making disciples in the twenty-first century as Jesus did in the first century. There is incredibly good news in this chapter, but we need to understand the bad news first.

WORLDVIEW

Del Tackett, president of the Focus Leadership Institute, described *worldview* as "the framework from which we view reality and make sense of life and the world."[2] In other words, worldview is what is real to us. Your perception of reality *is* reality to you. Your worldview is the set of tinted glasses through which you perceive reality. You get your worldview from family, friends, society, church, school, and all the social influences around you. Worldview is formed early in life and is difficult to change. I wish changing it were as easy as downloading an app for the iPhone, but instead we need a whole new operating system with new software.

Look at the following circle diagram and think about where you would start to transform someone's worldview into a biblical worldview.[3] We may attempt to address a person's behavior by aiming at the outside circle. We seem to feel that if people act "right" (according to our worldview's definition), they are more Christian. So we equate church attendance, Bible reading, giving, and serving in the church with discipleship—as Willow Creek Community Church did. If we are satisfied with changes in outward behavior only, Christianity becomes a veneer. The world calls that hypocritical. Another approach is to try to get people to value the "right" things and choose what is good—the second circle. This is better than just measuring behavior, but it can also be legalistic and become a facade. Millennials call that old-fashioned. The most common approach is to try to teach people the "right" beliefs — the third circle. Classes for new church members usually focus on beliefs. But if our beliefs are only religious dogma and do not challenge people's world of reality — their worldview — they fall short of transformation. Churches call this new member orientation. These partial approaches have led the world to think of many Christians as hollow. People don't believe that, at the core, we are real. We have mixed cultural Christian views with the world's views.

Next Generation

In U.S. society, a battle is under way for the souls of the next generation. Tom Gilson, in a review of the book *unChristian*, said,

> This book robbed me of sleep, revealing, as it does, how badly the church is disconnected from younger Americans, and how negatively we are viewed. The source of the disconnect, I'm convinced, is that our discipleship has been weak, sloganistic,

not very thoughtful, not loving enough, shallow. Though 29% of Americans say they are highly committed to Jesus Christ, only 3% espouse a Biblical worldview, defined for research purposes as adhering to 8 basic doctrines of Christian religion.[4]

A Barna study conducted among sixteen- to twenty-nine-year-old non-Christians shows that the next generation is "more skeptical of and resistant to Christianity than were people of the same age just a decade ago." For instance, a decade ago the vast majority of Americans outside the Christian faith, including young people, felt favorably toward Christianity's role in society. Currently, however, just 16 percent of non-*Christians* in their late teens and twenties said they have a good impression of Christianity.[5]

NEW REALITIES FOR EVANGELICALS

This Barna study shows that only 3 percent of sixteen- to twenty-nine-year-old non-Christians express favorable views toward *evangelicals*. This means that today's young non-Christians are eight times less likely to experience positive associations toward evangelicals than were non-Christians of the boomer generation (25 percent). Among young non-Christians, nine out of the top twelve perceptions were negative. Common negative perceptions include that present-day Christianity is judgmental (87 percent), hypocritical (85 percent), old-fashioned (78 percent), and too involved in politics (75 percent).[6]

However, this is not just those with a secular orientation; the Barna research shows that "millions of young outsiders have had significant experience with Christians and Christian churches. The typical young outsider says they have five friends who are Christians; more than four out of five have attended a Christian church for a period of at least six months in the past, and half have previously considered becoming a Christian."[7]

Perhaps that is part of the problem; they know Christians too well. Even churchgoing youth mirror the perceptions of their counterparts who are not Christians. "Half of young *churchgoers* said they perceive Christianity to be judgmental, hypocritical, and too political. One-third said it was old-fashioned and out of touch with reality."[8]

Shocking! Because of your worldview, you probably bristled, as I did, at some of the survey results. You probably began to defend yourself or your church because those comments conflict with your personal worldview. What they said is not reality for you.

What Happened?

The troubling truth is that we have failed to disciple our children and youth to a biblical worldview. We can give many answers to explain what happened, but the bottom line is that the world is doing a better job of discipling our children to popular culture than the church does in discipling them to Christ. Even more startling is the discovery that only one in nine evangelicals possesses a biblical worldview. That would be like only one member of a baseball team understanding the game. The percentage shrinks to one out of fifty evangelical teenagers who hold a biblical worldview.[9] These are our peers, our children, or our grandchildren!

Counter-Christian Culture

The U.S. culture is counter-discipling Christians using stories in films, videos, songs, and novels. Each week the typical adult spends an average of thirteen hours online compared to seven hours in 2002[10] and experiences emotional and riveting multimillion-dollar stories that stick in their hearts and minds. They find analogies and metaphors for their lives in these plots. They look for takeaways that they can use for bettering their lives. But at the same time they are being desensitized to God's name being taken in vain, promiscuous lifestyles of flawed characters, and the values of the world. Add to that the secularization of the school system, and you have a recipe for a godless society.

Young people are inundated with television, videos, the Internet, and other electronic media. Each year college students spend $6.5 billion on technology and an average of twelve hours a day interacting with some type of electronic media.[11] They absorb the messages from the media as if they were normal depictions of life. Today's generation shares videos on all topics through YouTube, Google Video, Vimeo, Videoegg, vSocial, and Grouper.[12] Videos become their reality shows. When young people need to make life choices, there is a predominance of flawed models from the world to choose from. Young people today are the "digital natives," and those of us who did not have all of this technology early in life are called "digital immigrants." Like anyone immigrating to a new country, we need to learn this new culture.

FROM THE WORLD'S WORLDVIEW TO GOD'S WORLDVIEW

The disciple-making process is essentially helping someone replace the nonbiblical portions of his or her worldview with a biblical worldview. But how do you change any part of a worldview? With a great deal of difficulty. Worldviews begin to be shaped when we are children, and we get our perceptions of reality from our parents, friends, peers, teachers, coaches, preachers, the Bible, and the society around us. Generally speaking, people adopt only the biblical values that they see exhibited in their models.

What chance do parents and Christian leaders have of counteracting this stream of non-Christian examples? Much better than you think. Noted theologian N. T. Wright said that the best way to change one's worldview is through better stories. The Bible has better stories to answer the issues of life than the world does.[13] Everything in this book points to how to attract, engage, and influence people for Christ. Authentic disciples who live what they believe, relate well to those who are not believers, care for people, and engage people in the Word of God in a natural way in real life are the kind of people that this skeptical generation is looking for. You have already read the stories of many whose worldview has been radically transformed. It is time to return to the biblical model and reclaim first-century discipleship in the twenty-first century. But we have to start with the core of each individual's worldview.

Truth: Absolute or Relative?

Gilles Gravelle works with The Seed Company, a Wycliffe U.S. affiliate organization; he lives in Seattle, Washington, and does storying through his church. He did a two-part series called "Truth and Postmodern Society" with middle-class high school students. He showed them a clip of the movie *The Passion of the Christ*, in which Pilate asks Jesus, "What is truth?" After discussing that question, he showed them a PowerPoint presentation with lots of graphics and pictures reviewing the history of the Enlightenment, modernism, and postmodernism to help them understand the context of the times they are living in and how they make rational choices.

Gilles led them to process the difference between objective and subjective truth in terms high school students would understand. He asked them to call subjective truth "ice cream" because it is personal preference and objective truth "insulin" because it is absolute and you have to have it to live.[14] The students practiced ways to identify the differences and did some fun things to experience what is relative and what is true for everybody. They discussed how the distinction between relative truth and absolute truth affects society as well as the results of the two ways of thinking about truth. Once they understood the problem, these concepts became real. Gilles asked them to look for examples of subjective and objective truth during the next week.

"They did!" Gilles exclaims. "I was surprised. They brought back all sorts of stuff." The students returned the next week with their lists of ice cream and insulin from their experiences at home, school, and church.

Gilles asked, "What is culture telling you about truth?" After hearing their answers, he told the story of Jesus' confrontation with the religious Jews (see John 8:31-48) very dramatically without opening his Bible. By using dialogue questions, he helped the students understand the plot twists and how Jesus had peeled away subjective truth with those around Him and revealed absolute truth. He shared a case study from his work among the Meyah-speaking people in Indonesia—how he had helped them strip away the lies of their taboos from reality. The students got it. They began using biblical knowledge to help differentiate the two types of truth (subjective and objective), rather than relying purely on their culturally influenced local worldview. It's not that students have rejected Christian values and truth as much as they have not understood them.

DISCIPLING TO THE CORE

Since the Lord can use stories to change someone's worldview, how do you pick the right stories and string them together in a set? Ah, there's the crunch. First, you have to understand the worldview of the group you are trying to reach. Muslims, Hindus, Buddhists, animists, and atheists all have very different worldviews. They disagree on where we came from, why we are here, what is right and wrong, where we are going in eternity, and how we can get there. In the United States we have many other worldviews depending on region, ethnic background, social status, educational experience, religion, and so forth. For example, the worldviews of an inner-city street kid, an immigrant, a Bible-belt southerner, an intellectual from the Northeast, a lifer in prison, and an abused person vary widely. To understand their worldview issues, you first learn all you can about them by getting to know them, asking the right questions, and doing research to help you understand their core worldview perspectives. This is not a call for impossible levels of research, but I am highly recommending a careful start in order to avoid erecting as many barriers as possible to the gospel's receptivity.[15] As you understand the worldview of the people you are dealing with, you can compare the bridges, barriers, and gaps in their worldview to a biblical worldview. Then you pick Bible stories that address each and ideally arrange them in a biblical chronology. There can be bridges, barriers, and gaps related to each circle of the worldview diagram on page 149.

Bridges

Bridge stories are ones that correspond to the worldview of others and make it easier for them to receive your message. For example, when we chose the stories from creation to Christ for Real Life Ministries, I said, "Since we are only telling thirty-four stories in nine months, we don't need the story of David and Goliath."

"Oh, no!" the staff replied. "You have to include that story. Remember who we are in northern Idaho. We are sportsmen and hunters, and we love competition. We have got to have David and Goliath to connect to these real men." I agreed.

Barriers

Barriers are obstacles that keep people from believing or accepting the biblical worldview. Sometimes barriers are obvious. Muslims do not believe Jesus rose from the dead, while Hindus believe that reincarnation means everyone eventually rises from the dead.

Barriers in Worldview

Barriers can also be subtle among people who may appear to be from the same culture. People from the southeastern part of Kentucky have an honor system that determines right or wrong — not the Bible. They have a long history of feuding, to the point that it has become a pattern that sociologists have come to believe was based largely on whether or not their European ancestors grew crops or shepherded animals. "The 'culture of honor' hypothesis says that it matters where you're from, not just in terms of where you grew up or where your parents grew up, but in terms of where your great-grandparents and great-great-grandparents grew up . . . That is a strange and powerful fact."[16]

If we are telling stories there, we would need to address the idea of defending one's honor by telling stories of Abraham, Jesus, and a number of other Bible heroes who lived differently — even turned the other cheek — when confronted by those who did not have a worldview based on the Bible.

— Mark

Gaps

Non-Christian worldviews have gaps where there is no concept — or a weak one — that corresponds to a biblical principle. These need to be addressed in the storying process. To a Muslim, that would mean telling stories about God's forgiveness. To a Hindu, stories about the nature of God and creation would be important. To a postmodern person, stories of what Jesus said and showed about absolute truth would be crucial in helping him or her understand a biblical worldview.

The key is to apply the right stories to the right people at the right time. We don't change the stories; we just wisely and intentionally choose the best ones for the people we are talking with.

A Model

Caesar Kalinowski moved to the Pacific Northwest to start Soma Church using a storying model. "In the Pacific Northwest, where it's much like Europe, sometimes you have post-Christian people. The café culture is cynical, fairly young, and fairly educated," he said. Caesar began by going to a café owner and suggesting they do a "story night." Anyone could tell any story he or she wanted, and some stories were pretty raunchy. However, Caesar, as the host, would listen for a theme from the stories and end by telling a Bible story that spoke to the issue others had raised. The patrons would listen intently, and then afterward individuals would come up and talk to him, and he would invite them to one of his storying groups. The church now has forty groups telling Bible stories to address the problems of life the people are facing. Caesar said, "Seattle is the most literate city in the nation. We have church plants all around. But the level of orality in our area is enormous. We need to speak in the cultural language of those around us. We have to address it as missionaries. We have to address it."[17]

Caesar said that one couple in his church experienced a real low point in their marriage when, in her mid-thirties, the wife decided she "was done with God." Her husband "tried everything," including forcing her to go to church.

"My wife and I went out with them as a couple," remembered Caesar. "She was awesome. Over time we built relational trust. We even had our missional-community [small-group] meeting at their home. She was a great hostess, but she'd go upstairs when the story started.

"Then we did 'The Story of God' in three nights. She was engaged from the start. She had killer questions. Her husband was shocked. In three nights she was transformed. Came to Sunday gatherings. We all said, 'What? What's going on?' She'd be like the first one whose hand would go up."

The woman was coming alive spiritually. Through attending a women's retreat, all the pieces came together for her. Caesar went on, "She spilled her guts about things bothering her. She became a believer, probably for the first time. She had never been able to piece all the stories together. From Genesis to Jesus she heard these stories, but never believed she measured up. She couldn't believe that God would actually forgive her sins—what she'd done. She thought that she couldn't get her questions answered. Through storying, stuff she wondered about came up in the dialogue."[18] God used stories from the Bible, personal relationships, and a loving group to draw her into a life-changing transformation.

God has given us a tool that hits the bull's-eye. Storying is incredibly relevant to this generation! The truth embedded in Bible stories can come alive for them. To disciple people at the core, we tell Bible stories that reshape their worldview by engaging them in the real issues of life.

In the next chapter, we'll see how this generation of unbelievers also responds when we pass on God's stories.

QUESTIONS FOR REFLECTION

1. What is worldview?
2. Where do we get our worldview, and how can it be changed?
3. Identify bridges, barriers, and gaps in your own or another's worldview.
4. Identify one or more stories from the Bible to address the bridges, barriers, and gaps of the worldview in the previous question.
5. Choose one worldview issue and look at the bridges, barriers, and gaps at each of the circles in the diagram: Knowledge, Values, Beliefs, Worldview.

CHAPTER 13

PASSING IT ON

One of the marks of the Christians of the first century was their spontaneity in telling everyone about Jesus. Peter and John said, "We cannot help speaking about what we have seen and heard" (Acts 4:20). Even when the disciples were chased out of town, "those who were scattered went on their way proclaiming the message of good news" (Acts 8:4, HCSB). Somehow in the twenty centuries since then, the majority of Christians have lost their spontaneous witness.

Using Bible Stories for Evangelism

One of the delightful discoveries in our adventures with storying is that people who learn Bible stories pass them on. Randy Proctor was trained in storying by the Great Commission Initiative group in Texas. He immediately put Bible storying to work the next week when he spoke to a five-week-old "cowboy church" in Oklahoma.

Randy told the Red Sea crossing story from Exodus as the cowboys and their families listened. "First I told the story as I had been taught—simply and unembellished," he recounted.[1] Then he asked several questions about the story.

Randy had to encourage the people to answer out loud—something new for them in church during the "preaching" time. In all, he asked about ten questions. Most of the time Randy got only brief answers, but he didn't push things. He relied on the Holy Spirit to move among the people who were considering what the crossing of the Red Sea meant to their lives. Who was holding them in bondage? What was pursuing them? Who was their "Pharaoh"? Who was their only hope of salvation?

Randy was slowly guiding them to a very special point. He finally had everyone stand up. "I asked them if they would surrender to God, asking Him to deal with the Pharaoh in their lives," Randy said. "I asked them to step to the front in response. Well, I lost count after fifteen stepped forward."

Randy asked if anyone would trust in Jesus to safely guide his or her life for all time. "Before I could finish the sentence," he said, "a woman in the back started waving both hands mouthing, '*I will, I will!*' I asked, 'Are there others?' Two more hands shot into the air. I asked, 'Are you also trusting Christ as Savior?' And they said, 'Yes! Yes!'"

Randy was amazed at how God had used this Bible story to bring people to faith in Christ. Afterward, one man spoke to him at the door and said, "Clearest Bible message I have ever heard in my life."

Pass It On!

When I returned from my fourteen years of experience with small home groups in Indonesia, I told Grady Cauthen, the president of the Baptist Sunday School Board (now LifeWay), "I believe that God is going to use small groups to reach America someday. We just have to wait for it to become culturally appropriate to do so."

As the culture has changed over the last quarter of a century, many non-Christians won't enter church buildings except for weddings and funerals, and even that practice is less and less frequent. But the good news is that today more non-Christians are open to meeting in friends' homes to talk about spiritual things. People are hungry for real relationships due to their isolation rooted in the proliferation of virtual technology.

I believe that God has brought us to a fullness of time in the twenty-first century to reach out to non-Christians by meeting in home groups and telling Bible stories with an open agenda where non-Christians feel comfortable. People can enter a Bible storying relational group at any point and feel that they can participate in listening to and telling stories and answering questions about them.

Open to Homes

In a 2006 study by LifeWay, the researchers discovered that of those who were "born again," 42.1 percent said they met weekly with a group of twenty or fewer people.[2] More revealing was the statistic that 26.3 percent of the 3,600 Americans polled indicated they met weekly in homes "as their *primary* form of spiritual or religious gathering" (emphasis added). Further, 63 percent of people currently not engaged in a local church "are willing to receive information about a local congregation or faith community from a family member, and 56 percent are willing to receive such information from a friend or neighbor."[3] What a great countermovement to the people we told you about in the last chapter who are distancing themselves from churches!

— Mark

It is not just Christian leaders who are spontaneously telling stories about Jesus. When the Real Life Ministries staff was experimenting with storying to see if it would work in their church, one of the community pastors was leading a group that grew to about thirty new people. Jeff, one of the group members, had tried without success to get one of his fellow employees to come to church. But when Jeff invited Scott to the home group, he decided to attend. Scott is a stonemason and has the physique to go with it — he is six feet two and weighs about 250 pounds. That first night, however, he was fidgety. The leader said, "Scott, you seem to be nervous."

"Yes," answered Scott hoarsely, "I've never been to a home group before, and you are a minister!"

"Don't let that bother you, Scott," the leader replied with a smile. "I'm just going to tell a story." He then told the story of Jesus getting into Peter's boat and inviting him to become a fisher of men (see Luke 5:1-11). The group went through the process of dialoguing about the story, and at the end the leader asked, "Who will tell this story next week when we begin our session?" The people were new, so they all ducked their heads.

Finally, Scott, who was not a believer, spoke up and said, "I'll tell it." That week he got his new Bible and practiced the story forty or fifty times on the job while he built stone fences. One of his fellow workers came with him to the next session just to see what happened next. To everyone's delight, Scott did a first-rate job telling the story that night.

But the clincher came the next week when Scott called the leader of the small group and said, "Well, I think I am ready to become a fisher of men." He got what Jesus was saying better than most people when they come to Christ.[4]

Pass It On!

God's stories are easily shared beyond the home-group experience. They "travel" much better than the outline on a church's bulletin insert or a fill-in-the-blank study guide. Stories talk!

Jim Blazin, home-groups pastor of Real Life Ministries, was called to the bedside of Terry, a terminally ill cancer patient. As they began to talk, Terry expressed his doubt that God could ever forgive him for all he had done to bring shame upon him and his family. Although Jim had his Bible with him, he felt it was far more appropriate to simply ask Terry and his wife if he could tell them a story from God's Word.

"Immediately Luke 15 came to mind—the story of the prodigal son," Jim said. "So I just storied the prodigal son to him. They both leaned in, and tears started coming from the wife's eyes and from his. The Word of God unlocked more understanding about God's grace for where Terry was in his season in life. God used it in a powerful way. I look back at that, and I think Terry thought that it was real to me and that I owned it and that it was part of who I was. And because of that, it was not confrontational to him. It was invitational. It was powerful."[5]

Pass It On!

In one home group the man whose turn it was to tell the story took it seriously. He started reading the story that night after it was assigned at the group meeting, and in a few days he began telling the story to his wife. His oldest son, who was seventeen and had "wandered from the faith" a few years before, asked him what he was doing. He told his son that he was practicing to tell the story in his home group the next week and was nervous about it.

The next night the man asked his son if he could practice the story on him, and he agreed. Every day before the meeting, he told the story to his son and had him correct him. This was a huge win to the man and his wife as they had been praying for their son for some time and had been unable to talk with him about God without conflict.

Finally the night arrived for the man to tell the story in the group. He asked his son if he wanted to come listen to him tell the story, and the son went. As the meeting began, the man got a crucial business call. He apologized and excused himself to take the call but was gone longer than expected. When he came back, he walked in on his son telling the story in his stead. The small-group leader saw him come in and winked at the man so he could let the son, who hadn't seen his father return, finish the story.

When the son finished, all the people, who knew how long the couple had prayed for him, praised him. Everyone participated in the dialogue led by the small-group leader. To the surprise of the man and his wife, their son answered several questions and obviously had thought a lot about the story. The next week the son asked if he could go to the home group again; he eventually gave his life to the Lord in the group.

PASSING IT ON TO YOUR FAMILY

Ed Young, pastor of Second Baptist Church in Houston, Texas, got my attention at a pastor's conference when he said, "I showed our denomination's statistics to a CEO and asked, if we were a business, what would he say about our condition. He said, 'You are going out of business.'" Ed displayed eight life-size cardboard cutouts of nineteen-year-old students standing behind him. Then one by one he called their names and pushed six of the eight figures over onto the floor. He said, "That is what is happening in our churches. We lose six out of eight of our students when they graduate from high school." How can we as Christians reverse that trend in our families?

FAMILY DEVOTIONS

I know by experience how to give our children a biblical worldview from which they can make good choices. My parents were devout Christians and conducted what they called "family devotions" every morning after breakfast—even on Saturday (regardless of whatever play plans we kids had). We would tell a Bible story or read a chapter of the Bible, sing a song, and then pray. At times my two sisters and I would act out stories, such as Daniel in the lions' den. I realized years later that although my dad was a powerful preacher, he had affected my life more through those fifteen-minute family devotions than with his preaching.

When Shirley and I began to have a family, we followed my parents' example. We had to change the time and format over the years to engage all of our children whose ages were spread over fourteen years (giving us nineteen straight years of teenagers). Most Christian children don't have the advantage of their parents regularly teaching them at home to follow God's commands. I am still haunted by the statistic that only 2 percent of evangelical teenagers have a biblical worldview.[6]

God taught Shirley and me how to give a biblical worldview to our children when He gave instructions to Israel as they were about to cross into the Promised Land:

Hear, O Israel: The LORD our God, the LORD is one. Love the LORD your God with all your heart and with all your soul and with all your strength. These commandments that I give you today are to be upon your hearts. Impress them on your children. Talk about them when you sit at home and when you walk along the road, when you lie down and when you get up. Tie them as symbols on your hands and bind them on your foreheads. Write them on the doorframes of your houses and on your gates. (Deuteronomy 6:4-9)

Note that Moses's tone is urgent and emotional. The words of God were to be repeated to children, talked about in the home and on travels, and kept in mind from sunup to sunset. They were to become as well known as the Israelites' hands and foreheads and as constantly visible as their doorposts and gates. But most of all, they were to be *in* their *hearts*.

The key was repetition. Repeat them, talk about them, bind them, and write them were all ways to have God's Word saturate their lives. Just as we attempted to pass God's Word on to our children, so our five children have taught their children; by the grace of God, all sixteen of our grandchildren are following Christ and serving God. The only one of our sixteen grandchildren who was not born in our family and is old enough to make a personal decision for Christ is Amy Marie, who was born in China and adopted by our son and his family when she was a year old. We visited them when she was three years old, and she told me about getting stuck by a thorn. I asked her, "Amy, do you know where thorns came from?"

"No, I don't know," she answered.

I asked, "Can I tell you the story of where thorns came from?" When she nodded yes, I began, "When God made the first man and the first woman . . ."

Amy interrupted me and said, "I know their names: Adam and Eve." Then she proceeded to tell me the story of the first man and woman! She hadn't been told about the thorns yet, but even a three-year-old can hide God's stories in her heart.

TELL ME THE STORY:
BRINGING THE BIBLE TO LIFE

With the publication of this book, Walk Thru the Bible and NavPress are introducing resources for you to give your children a biblical worldview. You can use the fifty-two recorded Bible stories called

Storying Thru the Bible: Bringing the Bible to Life with your family to address the worldview issues of our culture.[7] The recordings prepare parents to tell the story and then other family members to learn them. The accompanying book gives a simple "told" version of the story and introduces various experiential age-appropriate activities for the other days of the week. It also includes hand signs for each story that help listeners remember the stories in sequence and add new stories in chronological order. The stories are available on digital players called TruthSticks so that children can listen and learn them whenever they want and tell them to their friends.

The ideal process is for a church to plan a year or a school year of Bible storying in small groups from creation to Christ. Then parents can learn the stories in their small groups and use them with their families during the week (see Psalm 78:1-7). The small-group experience is key to preparing parents to share the Bible stories with their children without fear.

A different activity used in some home groups is that the children listen to the story with the adults and then a parent or young person takes the children into an adjoining room to work on a drama of the story while the adults dialogue about the story. At the close, the children come back and enact their drama of the story. Instructions for daily applications are included with the recorded stories with different activities for that day.

Pass It On!

Our ten-year-old granddaughter Kenna heard me tell a story at our church at Christmastime and then ask questions and involve the audience in dramatizing the story. Not long after she returned home to Colorado with her parents, she phoned me and told me this story.

"Granddad, I storied my friend to Christ this week," she began. When I asked her to tell me more she said, "I met this friend at school, and she had only heard the name of Jesus twice in her life. So I started telling her stories but not telling her they were from the Bible. I told her the stories of creation, Noah, and Jonah; then I told her they were from the Bible. She asked, 'Do you know any stories about girls?' So I told her the stories of Ruth and Esther.

"Then one day I brought my EvangeCube[8] to school. I showed it to her and asked if she was ready to receive Christ as her Lord and Savior, and she said, 'Yes.' So she accepted Christ in the line for recess. Then I asked her to explain the EvangeCube back to me, and she did. So now she is trying to lead her parents to Christ. I brought her a Bible, and we are reading through the New Testament."

When I saw Kenna a few months later, I asked her how far they had gotten in their Bible reading. Kenna said, "So far we are in John. Now I want to start an EvangeCube club for Christians at school. I am going to give them an EvangeCube and a Bible to tell the story at recess. And when kids come to Christ, I am going to give them an EvangeCube and a Bible for each person in their families. It's fun telling stories and leading people to Christ." About a month later another granddaughter in Indonesia, Mikayla, age nine, told me she had led her friend to Christ in the same way.

Pass It On!

One of the frequent criticisms of discipleship comes because some people think discipleship is only going deeper and deeper in the Word. We are seeing the TruthSticks strategy of making disciples in open home groups is the perfect place to bring unbelievers, involve them in fellowship, share Bible stories with them, and watch the Holy Spirit bring them to faith in Christ. Then they can share the stories with their families. It returns us to what Jesus did: make disciples and spread the Good News at the same time. May we see the way Jesus did it spread across America.

Pass it on!

QUESTIONS FOR REFLECTION

1. How could you use Bible storying to accelerate witnessing among the lost?
2. Why do Bible stories connect with those in the younger generations?
3. How can you give your children a biblical worldview?
4. What is your experience with teenagers leaving the church after high school?

CHAPTER 14

LASTING CHANGE

Our Iceberg Is Melting is a delightful parable on change written by John Kotter, the leadership and change guru at Harvard Business School, in collaboration with Holger Rathgeber. It tells the story of a colony of 260 penguins who live on an iceberg. A mid-level penguin named Fred spots cracks in the ice; he realizes that the iceberg is melting and the whole colony is in danger of losing its home. In the story Fred enlists other penguins to help make decisions that radically change the colony's situation for the better. The book follows the eight steps of the change process that Kotter spelled out in his management book *Leading Change.*[1]

We have detailed the urgent situation of the church in America. But you also know that change is not easy. As you consider how you can lead your church or small group to implement the changes that need to be made, you may be asking the basic questions that anyone beginning a new venture asks. The questions of "How broad? How deep? How long? How far?" need to be faced whether you are starting an around-the-world trip in a sailboat, launching a new business, starting a new organization, or reinventing the way you do things.

As you consider implementing what we have discovered together, you may be asking: "Is Bible storying a valid strategy for evangelism and discipleship or just a fad that will last awhile and then fade away? Is this a method I'll only use occasionally? Is this strategy sustainable over the long haul? What difference will this make in the long run? Is this a lasting change?"

Only two things are eternal: the Bible and people. We put them together when we use the Bible to make disciples.

How Broad?

How broad you go with discipleship affects personal transformation, biblical comprehension, and practical application. Let me tell you a story!

Pearl Collinsgrove became a Christian at age seventy-nine. She had grown up with her parents doing vaudeville and had only finished the third grade; by age seventy-nine, she had become blind. She began studying *MasterLife* after she heard some of her friends talk about experiencing life in Christ. Because of Pearl's blindness and limited education, some church members thought she would not be able to participate in the *MasterLife* group. Nevertheless, one member recorded the materials on audiotapes for Pearl. She quickly memorized all of the Scripture verses and the major presentations. Composers had created songs for each of the fifty-two memory verses in the original *MasterLife*. Pearl loved these songs, and, as a former entertainer, she began singing her memorized Scripture verses as she played her guitar. Civic clubs around town invited her to speak and sing. A group member made her a large *MasterLife* Disciple's Cross that sums up the Christian life. When she spoke, she held that full-size cardboard cross in front of her and explained that she was now abiding in Christ; then she sang a song based on John 15:5 that related to the center of the cross and telling her story.

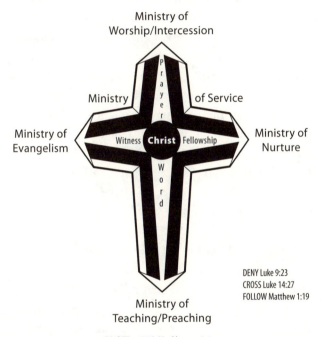

©LifeWay, 1996. Used by permission.

As she gave the visual signs, she explained, "My feet are planted in God's Word; my hands are lifted up to heaven in worship and prayer; one hand reaches out to my Christian brothers and sisters in fellowship; and the other hand reaches out to the lost world that we need to tell about Jesus." Then she sang the memory verses related to each point of the Disciple's Cross. Word spread about Pearl's testimony, and to rousing applause she sang John 15:5 at a meeting of 45,000 Christians in Dallas, Texas. Nothing—age, blindness, lack of education—could deter this fervent woman from holding firm to the Word of God and sharing her story![2]

Pearl was a visible example of a discipling process that I spent twenty-five years developing as a pastor, missionary, and denominational discipleship leader. I only wish I had known about Bible storying then, because it would have been even more effective in Pearl's life and allowed her to share the full story with others better.

I mention the *MasterLife* process because it comprehensively and systematically covers the biblical discipleship content and important life issues. *MasterLife* is still being used around the world with the same effectiveness among literate learners thirty years after I translated it from Indonesian to English. But you might be asking, "Can Bible storying be that comprehensive? How much of the truth will oral-preference disciples know, and how deep can they go in understanding and using the Word, experiencing life change, and persevering in time of trouble?" The TruthSticks strategy uses the same biblical discipling patterns that go broad and deep.

FOLLOWING JESUS

The eight storytellers I assembled after my return from Amsterdam in 2000 used the *MasterLife* discipling process as a guide and recorded more than four hundred Bible stories dealing with discipleship and leadership in the *Following Jesus* audio series. For example, *Following Jesus* presents Bible stories covering every point in the Disciple's Cross diagram, from living in Christ all the way to equipping disciples as ministers and multiplying leaders.

This discipleship process lasts because it focuses on the relationship with Christ (at the center of the cross). Picture the process spiraling out from the center of the circle as the participants use practical applications every day of the four disciplines on the crossbars of the cross. As they know God better and serve people, they naturally flow into the practice of the ministries on the perimeter of the points on the cross. By the time disciples have grown through this discipling process, either as literates or oral learners, they have established lifelong patterns of going deeper in interpretation and application of the Word in their lives. Many oral learners get so engaged in the process that they have worked on their reading proficiency in order to use the literate tools available to others.

Real Life Ministries has conducted more than one hundred *MasterLife* groups to train its leaders and take them further in their development as spiritual leaders. Literally every week, and wherever I go in the world, I meet people and hear testimonies of lasting life changes through this discipleship process.

HOW DEEP? HOW FAR?

Someone may challenge you if you begin using Bible stories, saying, "Storying will not take you deep enough or far enough." You don't have to worry about not having enough curricula to engage people and take them as far as the Lord intends when you use the stories of the Bible. Although I am not prescribing the exact stories in *Following Jesus: Making Disciples of Oral Learners* as your curriculum, if you used one story a week, you would have enough to last eight years. The stories help develop disciples, taking people who have never heard of Christ all the way to becoming pastors and missionaries. No need to worry about going deep enough or far enough!

For example, the first module of *Following Jesus* includes a training course in storying, but the second module consists of sixty-five chronological Bible stories—from creation to Revelation—to give people a biblical worldview. In this case, we decided to choose stories that would address the worldview of Mandarin-speaking Chinese people. We expect people using these stories for other social and ethnic groups to choose the stories that address the bridges, barriers, and gaps in the worldview of the hearers (see chapter 12).

In the seven modules, disciples learn thirty stories that characterize discipleship and cover the basics of the Disciple's Cross. As they mature in Christ, they learn ten stories related to the Ten Commandments and nine stories about Jesus related to the nine fruit of the Spirit. They also learn stories to help them overcome barriers to spiritual growth, such as money, sex, and pride.

Believers learn how to minister and do spiritual warfare in all the areas mentioned around the points of the Disciple's Cross. These are followed by stories on how to multiply disciples and equip spiritual leaders. The seventh module equips believers to become missionaries. This module was done at the request of the Chinese Christians' Back to Jerusalem Movement, which plans to send 100,000 missionaries from China through the Middle East Muslim nations on the way back to Jerusalem. Thousands of these four hundred–plus audio stories in Mandarin have been distributed in China as well as translated into other languages used in China.

My purpose in listing these resources is to show that you can choose stories to meet the needs of people you are working with at any point in their lives and to deal with any worldview or theological issue you need to address, no matter how comprehensive and deep. It is best for you to choose the stories that meet the worldview issues of your people rather than simply using this set. Let it serve as a library and a model that you creatively change to relate to the issues your people face.

Going Deeper

Jim and Janet Stahl work with The Seed Company, an affiliate of Wycliffe Bible Translators. Their pastor at First Presbyterian Church in Duncanville, Texas, asked them to tell Bible stories to their adult Sunday school class that would parallel the next sermon series. They faced a real problem when they realized the pastor was planning the series on Galatians!

To help people understand the bigger story around Galatians, they told the stories of Stephen and his martyrdom, Paul's conversion, and Peter's experience with Cornelius from the book of Acts. Then they told Paul's five arguments in Galatians built on the way Paul used pairs in each argument. At first, there was some resistance in the class of about thirty people because they said stories were for children.

However, it was such a lively class that the Stahls' role was reduced to guiding the dialogue. The members who had been so resistant realized how powerful storying could be and asked, "Why have we never done this before?"[3]

— Avery

Should you use Bible storying exclusively? Probably not with people who read well. In fact, the storying process causes people to want to study the Bible more. For most of us in America, these two approaches are more like the two blades of scissors: One is more effective when used with the other. But we don't want to leave out people who won't, don't, or can't read because of the means we use to communicate with them.

How Long?

How long do you use stories and with whom? The more pertinent question is how long will the problem of people not reading or being able to read effectively persist? The problem defines how long the process is needed. So you need to use these stories as long as people don't read or remember the Bible and as long as the stories are effective.

The National Assessment of Adult Literacy conducted by the U.S. Department of Education in 2003 affirmed that essentially the same percentage of people had inadequate reading skills as in its 1992 landmark study, even though billions of dollars had been spent to improve education during that period.[4] We must not postpone communicating the gospel or making disciples until people's reading skills are good enough to use literate materials. Neither can we wait until the motivation of literates to read books improves. The problem will not go away.

The first half of this book showed that God created us to learn through stories, dialogue, drama, poetry, song, repetition, and sharing. It's the way we were made and the way people have learned since the beginning of time. No matter how well we learn literate methods, they do not negate the natural ways we learn best. The more we use interactive learning methods, the better our disciples learn and reproduce.

How Well?

The National Training Laboratories (NLT), in Bethel, Maine, reports results from research projects on a variety of learning methods where knowledge was best retained.[5] Virtually all the methods apply to the way that we use Bible storying in small groups to help people grow as oral-preference learners.

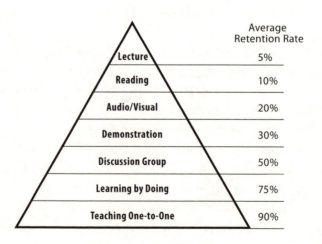

Learning Pyramid
National Training Laboratories, Bethel, Maine

	Average Retention Rate
Lecture	5%
Reading	10%
Audio/Visual	20%
Demonstration	30%
Discussion Group	50%
Learning by Doing	75%
Teaching One-to-One	90%

The least effective method used to communicate information (measured by retention) is hearing a lecture (5 percent). Reading doubles retention to 10 percent. Audiovisual methods double learning again to 20 percent. If people see a demonstration, they retain 30 percent of the information they received (think dramatizing stories); if they discuss it, the percentage moves to 50 percent (think dialogue). When people learn content by doing (application), the percentage retained goes to 75 percent. When you add the one-to-one component, learning and retention rise to an astounding 90 percent (think discipleship). Using all of the methods makes truth stick.[6]

ONE-ON-ONE

Jesus discipled His disciples in real-life situations as a group, but when He wanted to deal with problems and make sure one of the disciples got the message, He would talk to him one-on-one. Peter is the most obvious recipient of this one-on-one treatment, both because he needed it and because Jesus was training him to lead the disciples after Jesus ascended. Jesus coached Peter for life change when He invited him to walk on the water, when He rebuked Peter for telling Jesus that He would not die, when He told Peter that he was going to deny Him, and when He asked Peter if he loved Him after his denial of Jesus.

One-on-one coaching works today just as it did with Peter. Darren Owens was living with his girlfriend, Melina, in Post Falls when he received a flier that Real Life Ministries was meeting in a movie theater. Jim Putman, the pastor, remembered what happened a few months after Darren and Melina joined his small group. "I went to him and said, 'Darren, I've got to talk to you about this living arrangement you are in.' I went to his house, and we talked about what the Bible said about marriage."

Darren got it. He said, "Okay, we need to separate and then get married."

They separated until they could get married. A few months later, the church was growing rapidly, and when they needed additional small-group leaders, Jim went back to Darren and asked if he would lead a group.

"I've only been saved not very long, and I just got married a couple months ago, and I don't know anything!" Darren said.

"You know, here's the deal, dude," Jim said. "You were committed enough to the Lord that you did what you said you would and got married. You got right with Him. I don't expect you to know everything, but here's what we are going to do. You are going to start meeting with me on Wednesday mornings. We will go through the lesson; then Wednesday night you're going to lead a small group. Then you're going to come back, and we will debrief what happened. If you don't know the answer, say, 'I don't know, but I'll know by next week.'"

Darren agreed, and their relationship went to the next level. When Darren didn't know the answer to a question, he went back to Jim. From that point on, Darren made significant strides toward spiritual maturity. He became an apprentice small-group leader and in the next year began leading a new group. He eventually became a coach over several home groups. Today as a Real Life Ministries staff member, Darren serves as a community pastor overseeing fifty small groups and is making plans to plant a new church.[7]

Implementing Change in Your Church

At Real Life Ministries, we have had to make several changes in order to grow as fast as we have in just ten years. We knew that moving to storying in our home groups would be a monumental change, so we took our time. First, the executive staff was trained and started using storying in their small groups. Next, the community pastors were trained, followed by the training of coaches, who were responsible for several small groups.

We formed focus groups of influential small-group leaders to talk about the possibility of making a change to storying. Then, we gathered all the small-group leaders together to train them and answer their questions. We accepted their feedback with appropriate and timely responses. We insisted on going at our small-group leaders' pace — not forcing them into a commitment — and relationally working with many individuals until finally we were ready to implement the new storying curriculum.

It was a huge success right from the beginning! We shared our experiences with each other and celebrated what God led us to do in our church. Now, it is part of our culture, and our people are leading the way on how to do a better job telling the stories of the Bible in small groups.[8]

— Brandon Guindon

BEGINNING WITH THE END IN MIND

So how do you start so that you go far enough, long enough, and deep enough to make disciples? After you get buy-in from the leaders, it is best to begin by using a set of Bible stories in chronological order to convey the redemptive panorama from Genesis to Revelation. Most believers in America today do not know the sequence of God's story and therefore do not have a biblical worldview.

After my first year of training the pastors, coaches, and small-group leaders with Real Life Ministries, we identified issues that hindered their church members from developing a biblical worldview. We chose thirty-four Bible stories that would address these issues and arranged them in chronological order in *Following Jesus Together*. The church and their mission churches used the stories in their small groups for the next year.

By the time I started the third year of consulting with Real Life

Ministries, I was intrigued by the idea of telling the New Testament stories of Jesus' interactions with His disciples in the timeline of His ministry. I wondered what we would learn about becoming disciples and making disciples by following them chronologically through the Gospels. I worked with the church staff to have them identify which stories from the life of Jesus would be most applicable to the discipleship issues of their seven thousand small-group members.

The *Following Jesus: Making Disciples of Oral Learners*[9] audio series of more than four hundred stories can serve as a guide if you want to develop other sets of discipleship stories to ensure you cover all the bases in discipleship. The following year Real Life Ministries developed its own set of stories from the book of Acts and plans to continue developing contextualized curriculum for its small groups.

You can go as deep as you want, as far as you want, and as long as God leads you in making disciples using the stories of the Bible. An intentional discipler using Bible storying in a relational small group with a reproducible process for spiritual growth produces disciples who are "walking and talking Bibles."

QUESTIONS FOR REFLECTION

1. How deep can you go in your walk with the Lord using Bible storying?
2. How long are you willing to spend in each stage of spiritual development?
3. How far are you willing to go to make sure that critical discipleship issues are addressed in your life, your church, and your community?
4. What would be the best strategy to use for your church to move to Bible storying in small groups?[10]

CHAPTER 15

MULTIPLYING

Throughout this book, I have told you my personal story of how God led me to the TruthSticks strategy. You remember Marcus Vegh asking me, "How do you make disciples of oral learners?" And my struggle is certainly not unique.

What I did not tell you was that Steve Douglass was facilitating our group discussion at table 71 at that Billy Graham Amsterdam 2000 meeting. Steve had just been elected to succeed Bill Bright as the president of Campus Crusade for Christ International and was not looking for anything else to do. As Steve led our group to discuss how to reduce the number of unreached people groups in the world to zero, he excitedly said, "Let's just do it! The organizations represented here have enough people and money to do that."

No longer could we settle for methods that just *added* disciples to the kingdom. Making disciples in the hardest places in the world—crossing the challenging religious, cultural, and political barriers—would take *multiplication*.

Table 71 members, representing the largest missions agencies in the United States, have met three times a year since 2000 and have helped spawn several global initiatives. During one meeting I shared with them about our work on the *Following Jesus: Making Disciples of Oral Learners* audio series. We invited Jim Slack, a chronological Bible storying pioneer and one of our eight storyers, to present the facts about 70 percent of the unreached people groups being oral learners.

Steve explained, "When I got exposed to orality at Table 71, I said, 'Wow!' but I was just thinking about *primary* orality." The member organizations of Table 71 became the core of the Orality Issues work group for the Lausanne Committee on World Evangelization originally started by Billy Graham to influence the evangelical world in evangelism.[1] This orality work group wrote the landmark book *Making Disciples of Oral Learners* and birthed the International Orality Network (ION). Through these efforts Steve realized he could apply storying to groups other than nonreaders living overseas. "It dawned on me that students in colleges thought like this too. I knew no statistics to support this. I just experienced that it was true."

Despite his day job as president of Campus Crusade for Christ, Steve started discipling University of Central Florida students using storying in 2005. His original two groups grew to eight groups within four months. When they finished the twelve planned sessions, Steve agreed to work through one more set of lessons and created one-page leader guides for each session. Students from the original two groups began leading their own groups. A year later, twenty-one groups had formed, and by February 2007, there were thirty-five groups involving 290 students. Since then these groups have spread to more than forty campuses.[2]

WHY MULTIPLICATION?

Multiplication is God's idea, and He expects it to take place. He told the first man and woman, "Be fruitful" (Genesis 1:28). He told Abraham, "Count the stars. . . . So shall your offspring be" (Genesis 15:5). In the parable of the sower, Jesus said, "Still other seed fell on good soil, where it produced a crop—a hundred, sixty or thirty times what was sown" (Matthew 13:8). Bob Buford, author of *Halftime*, said that he wanted "100 Times" to be on his tombstone because he had been the "good soil" and multiplied himself at least one hundred times.[3]

Jesus told His disciples, "I chose you and appointed you to go and bear fruit—fruit that will last" (John 15:16). His final mandate to the disciples was to "make disciples of all nations" (Matthew 28:19), and the record of the first church says they did exactly that. "And the word of God increased; and the number of the disciples multiplied in Jerusalem greatly" (Acts 6:7, KJV). And "then had the churches rest throughout all Judaea and Galilee and Samaria and . . . were multiplied" (Acts 9:31, KJV).

Multiplication of disciples follows the natural pattern God established for families in Genesis 1:26-28. I asked my grandfather, age ninety-six, and my grandmother, age eighty-nine, how many descendants they had. "Sixty-two," my grandmother answered quickly.

For fun I asked, "My, Granny, how did you raise them all?"

"I didn't raise them all, thank goodness!" she exclaimed with a chuckle. "I just raised six of them."

"What about the rest?"

"Well, I helped some on the nineteen grandchildren; I changed your diapers. But I didn't do much on the thirty-five great-grandchildren or the two great-great-grandchildren. Their parents took care of them."

Multiplication happens when we make disciples who make disciples. The TruthSticks strategy described in this book will multiply for a lifetime with groups that are open to new participants who visit whenever the small group meets.

MULTIPLYING DISCIPLES

Gene Jacobs, a man of slender build and a chiseled look from years serving in the Navy and building communications towers, said that his first small-group experience at Real Life Ministries was, well, loud. A woman had invited Gene and his wife, Christy, to the group separately, not knowing they were on the verge of divorcing. When they showed up, there were eighteen adults and forty kids trying to meet in a double-wide trailer.

"We got to see couples come to home group fighting," remembered Gene. "Now from my background as a little kid, I know what happens when people fight like that—they get divorced. And I think most Americans would agree that's the typical response. But we got to see people loving on these folks—men taking the men aside, women taking the women aside, and praying together and walking with them as they tried to restore their marriage."[4]

Gene and Christy not only patched up their own marriage but also began sharing their faith in the workplace. Their home-group leader took notice and expressed interest in having Gene become his apprentice. Two weeks later, Gene took over the leadership of a new small group.

Multiplying Disciples in Prison

Paul Krueger and Chuck Broughton from the Navigators have worked for six years to bring Bible storying to the inmates at the Louisiana State Penitentiary at Angola, once known as the bloodiest prison in America. The prison is the size of Manhattan Island and has 5,200 prisoners. More than 80 percent of its inmates are there for life with no chance of parole.

These Navigators were asked by Burl Cain, the warden, to bring their audio discipleship program to the prison. Chuck had created twenty lessons at an elementary reading level that included Bible stories as well as several Bible verses recorded on MegaVoice players, which are solar-powered and use microchips like MP3 players.

"It's a good place to try new things," said Paul. "Nobody's going anywhere." Today in Angola, the groups have multiplied to twenty-eight churches and a totally internal two-year Bible college.

There are 142 inmates who have been through the storying process. Several of them became chaplains and have been transferred to other prisons. The warden transfers inmate chaplains in groups of three to give support as they enter a new prison and expand their ministries.

"Yes, you can do discipleship in prison," Paul says. "There are biblical truths that need to be delivered on a bridge of love. We keep it simple. We use stories."[5]

—Mark

MULTIPLYING HERE AND THERE

Real Life Ministries had already been involved in overseas ministry before they started using Bible storying, but their eyes were opened to how a local church can have a world ministry that is effective. Jim Putman said, "Bible storying works here *and* overseas. We discovered that what we had done in our small groups prepared us to minister in Ethiopia. Brandon Guindon, our executive pastor, used to be our small-groups guy. He took us from twelve groups to 650 groups. He went to Ethiopia to support Duane and Jackie Anderson, two of our small-group leaders who became medical missionaries."

Dr. Anderson runs a hospital in Ethiopia and invited Brandon and a man we'll call Bill (who leads a medical ministry in Illinois) to help his doctors become small-group disciplers. Bill argued against using Bible storying. He said, "This won't work. This will cause heresy. Who knows how they are going to tell the story? The story is going to change because they don't have a Bible to check it." And so on. However, he watched Brandon model it while they were in Ethiopia.

A year later when Jim, Brandon, Bill, and his wife returned to Ethiopia, they found that the oral methods were working in wonderful ways. And, of all things, Bill's wife started the first training session with the leaders by storying Nehemiah!

Brandon pulled Bill aside and asked him, "Bill, what's going on? You violently opposed storying last year, and now your wife is storying? What gives?"

Bill responded, "Oh, I know. I went back to my men's breakfast Bible group in Illinois. They are mechanics and regular Joe Blow guys, and since it's always me talking, they never opened up. So I decided to try it. The first time I told a story—the very first time—the guys started opening up and sharing. I asked a guy if he wanted to tell the story next week, and the guy for the first time said yes. Well, since that time the group has branched and branched. And I have won people to the Lord by telling stories."

Jim remarked, "So now, in one year's time he has become our biggest proponent for Bible storying in Ethiopia!" Jim was quick to point out that Dr. Anderson's influence has extended to other small groups. "Several of our small-group members go over there every year. Another one of our coaches who started in a small group became an apprentice, became a leader, and now he's a coach. He regularly takes teams over to Ethiopia. We have several who have become, as that doctor has become, missionaries at this point. And they started out just going to a small group."

Serving in Ethiopia in a hospital has its challenges, but Dr. Anderson has begun seeing fruit. I got a personal phone call from Jim Putman recently. He said that three Ethiopian sheiks (Muslim leaders) had come to faith in Christ. Shane and Allyson Smith, colleagues of the Andersons, reported that these men, representing a hundred other sheiks, "keep telling us that they don't want money or anything from us; they just want Bible training because they can share their testimonies, but they don't know enough to teach. They keep saying that they want to 'grow up' [mature] in Christ and that if we will just train them, they will take the gospel throughout Africa since they are respected, know Arabic, and are experts in the Koran."[6] I was able to link them to some International Mission Board missionaries who had developed storying training for people with their worldview.

MULTIPLYING GROUPS

On the home front, Jim Blazin, home-groups pastor of Real Life Ministries, said, "We have a bunch of leaders who are taking their apprentices or someone in their groups to go minister to other people—believers and unbelievers. We are averaging probably sixteen baptisms a week here. The Word is being sown into their hearts, and it's translating into fruit."

Gene Jacobs, the discipler mentioned on page 186, is a good example. He led a home group for several months. Brandon Guindon worked with Gene to help him develop his own apprentices and begin forming more new small groups. After branching to start three new groups over several months, Gene was asked to become a coach and be responsible for several small-group leaders.

One day Brandon asked if they could go camping in the woods to give them time for a serious talk. Brandon offered Gene a position on the Real Life Ministries church staff. Considering his background, his former marital troubles with Christy, and his rapid rise through their member-apprentice-leader-coach system, Gene was surprised by the invitation.

"I expected to hear angels and all these amazing things to happen," said Gene, "but instead I'm standing there with Brandon eating scrambled eggs in the middle of the woods, with him asking me to pray about it." Gene accepted the challenge to serve as a community pastor for Real Life Ministries.[7]

MULTIPLYING LEADERS

Jim Putman said the most-frequently asked question when churches come to Immersion (Real Life Ministries' training for church staff members) is "Where did you get all these leaders?"

Jim replied, "We grew them. Eighty-five of the ninety people on our church staff came right out of the community. We took them through the reproducible disciple-making process, and when they were ready—and sometimes before they thought they were ready—we put them on the 'playing field' as apprentices, small-group leaders, coaches, and community pastors. They often were diamonds in the rough, but weren't Jesus' disciples?"

Jim continued, "I like orality because it helps me produce leaders. The number one thing I hear when I ask a person to lead a small group is 'I don't know enough.' Why? Because they have in mind that old model that says, 'I have to have all the answers.' But when I ask them, 'Can you tell a story and ask questions?' they say, 'Of course, I can do that.' It gives them a place to play and develop. Then everyone in the group learns to tell the stories. It gives them a tool for their toolkit. They may not be able to quote verses, but they can tell a story to witness or talk to an unbeliever. It also helps them disciple their kids. By becoming an apprentice to the small-group leader, they get a place to try out their growing skills. When they become small-group leaders, they have a place to grow and to develop their skills."[8]

Jim said that he once talked with a pastor who started a church about the same time that Real Life Ministries was planted. Jim learned that the pastor had met with twenty-three men for eighteen months.

Jim was surprised to hear that at the end of that time, the pastor did not think any of the men were ready to be released to put the training into practice. Jim gave the pastor a small piece of paper and asked him to write down everything he thought they still needed to know. The pastor wrote for several minutes, filling up that piece of paper and several other sheets. To Jim, it looked like the outline for a seminary master's degree program. Jim pointed out that the pastor's philosophy was not only a hindrance to his men, but it was affecting the church's ability to grow. Jim told the pastor, "You expect things of your team that Jesus didn't expect of His (like a Bible college degree). If you require your team to know all those things, most of them will never feel good enough to disciple others." Some eight years later, that church has only one hundred members, and the pastor has had to train a new group of men. The others left because they felt "overwhelmed and unworthy."[9]

MULTIPLYING CHURCHES

Real Life Ministries has started five churches in the surrounding area; each has from 200 to 2,500 people attending. All of them use storying methodology in relational small groups. Gene and Christy Jacobs heard that Real Life Ministries was considering planting a new church forty-five miles and two serious mountain passes away in Silver Valley, Idaho. The town used to be wealthy until the mines ran out. Poverty set in, and it is now a U.S. government cleanup site. Gambling and prostitution are rampant.

The Jacobses joined four Real Life Ministries members who had been commuting to Post Falls from Silver Valley. Gene told them to invite everyone they knew, and they had forty people attend their first church service. Soon they had several small groups going.

Gene originally had been skeptical about Bible storying as a way to make disciples. In fact, he called it "the dumbest thing I ever heard of." However, while serving at Real Life Ministries, he quickly saw the advantages of storying and embraced it.

Gene said, "Here was part of the struggle. During our seven years of small groups, we tried everything to get God's Word into people's hearts. The amazing thing when we started doing storying is how well you pay attention to God's Word when you might have to tell the story in front of your friends."[10]

So when Gene went to Silver Valley, storying in small groups was something he just did naturally. He started a home group with seventeen attending, trusting that the Lord would move and the people would respond. They did. Chris Meyer, a firefighter, accepted Christ and was the first to be baptized. Another was Jordan White, a roofer, who often tells Bible stories on the job. These men are now leading their own groups and making disciples who follow Jesus.

After six months, Gene, Christy, and their daughter moved to Silver Valley, and Gene has successfully planted his first church, with 350 attending. Gene is now fully into the multiplying mode—both churches and people. The church has a goal to double the ten small groups that were active as of June 2009. As Gene says with a twinkle in his eye that reflects the love and zeal in his heart, "It's our valley."[11]

Is Gene Jacobs's story totally unique and impossible to replicate? We believe it is achingly normal for a church to multiply when disciple making is the chief priority. And normal enough to serve up as a model for investing in people who—like Gene, Christy, Chris, and Jordan—can participate in spiritual reproduction.

MULTIPLYING MISSIONS

Today, Real Life Ministries has multiplied its ministry across the nation through monthly training seminars called Immersion I, Immersion II, and Boot Camp for Church Planters. It has also sent teams and missionaries to Mexico, Peru, Ethiopia, Zimbabwe, China, and beyond.

Jim Putman pointed out that churches often talk about going into the world to make disciples, but they fail. Getting people off the side-lines and into the game, such as Gene Jacobs' story reflects, is the key.

"I want it to become a movement that is released rather than something that is controlled," Jim told us. "I just want people to make disciples."[12]

One missionary working with the Maasai people in Kenya arranged for several church teams to come to reach the older people who had not followed the example of the young warriors who had believed. The missionary had each team learn ten stories[13] to tell, and he coordinated these teams so they covered the whole story from creation to Christ. As a result, the older Maasai men respected the gray-haired volunteers and followed Christ.[14]

I started this book telling you how I learned to use oral strategies overseas with primary oral learners and have seen it spread around the world. You can read some of the stories in *Making Disciples of Oral Learners* and *Orality Breakouts: Using Heart Language to Transform Hearts*. Here is just one example that illustrates the before and after effects of Bible storying training. The results of a one-year effort by the Simply the Story project in south India were startling. Before they were trained in oral methods, the 50 nonliterate people took an average of 2.7 years to lead 815 people to Christ and plant 22 churches. After the 50 nonreaders were trained to tell 85 stories, they led 9,122 people to Christ and planted 370 churches in *one year*.[15] God's truth had stuck like Velcro and transformed lives!

Multiplication is God's idea—here, there, and everywhere!

QUESTIONS FOR REFLECTION

1. When it comes to making disciples, what is the difference in the process between *adding* new disciples and *multiplying* new disciples?

2. Why do you think it is impossible to multiply groups, churches, and missions without multiplying disciples first?

3. How are leaders multiplied?

4. Why does God continue to bless methods that multiply disciple making around the world?

THE FUTURE IS NOW

Our journey together has produced a collage of images. We started with a promise to show you how to make truth stick like Velcro in a Teflon world. We took you through the process of putting the pieces of a storying and discipleship puzzle together until the whole picture was in place. We introduced you to the image of the DNA of first-century discipleship that could be reclaimed in the twenty-first century. We summed up the whole process with the name TruthSticks, which represented the complete process.

Early in Jesus' ministry, even He found that it was not easy to make truth stick with His disciples. He was amazed that the disciples did not understand the truth or remember it. For example, He asked the disciples,

> You of little faith, why are you talking among yourselves about having no bread? Do you still not understand? Don't you remember the five loaves for the five thousand, and how many basketfuls you gathered? Or the seven loaves for the four thousand, and how many basketfuls you gathered? How is it you don't understand that I was not talking to you about bread? But be on your guard against the yeast of the Pharisees and Sadducees. (Matthew 16:8-11)

Nevertheless, by the end of His ministry, He was able to trust that the Holy Spirit would bring it all together at the right time for them. "Whenever you are arrested and brought to trial, do not worry beforehand about what to say. Just say whatever is given you at the time, for it is not you speaking, but the Holy Spirit" (Mark 13:11).

The reality is that truth *did* stick. Two of the Twelve wrote gospel accounts recording the things He did and the words He said. And scholars believe that Peter dictated the gospel of Mark to John Mark, who wrote it down. In addition, Peter wrote two epistles based on his experiences with Jesus. The apostle Paul dictated many of his epistles to his helpers, who wrote them to the churches. He confidently told his disciple Timothy, "And the things you have heard me say in the presence of many witnesses entrust to reliable men who will also be qualified to teach others" (2 Timothy 2:2).

But Paul summed up our hope for this book when he said,

> You yourselves are our letter, written on our hearts, known and read by everybody. You show that you are a letter from Christ, the result of our ministry, written not with ink but with the Spirit of the living God, not on tablets of stone but on tablets of human hearts. (2 Corinthians 3:2-3)

From a prison in Louisiana to churches in Washington and Idaho over to South Carolina and more than forty-five college campuses in between, small groups that story the Bible are making disciples who multiply themselves. TruthSticks will come alive for you when you put it into practice with real people in real groups. It is more caught than taught. If you are able do it in the environment of a disciple-making church, the impact is exponential.

A CALL FOR A REVOLUTION

We challenge you to begin a disciple-making revolution in your sphere of influence using the DNA of the first-century church in the twenty-first century. God is calling us back to His model for making truth stick. We call this concept "DNA21: Reclaiming First-Century Discipleship in the Twenty-First Century." DNA21 is a discipleship revolution that sums up all we are talking about in *Truth That Sticks*.

A majority of Christians in the twenty-first century are not experiencing the basic elements that enabled the first-century disciples to take Christ to the known world in their lifetimes. Human DNA is as old as creation, but only in the last fifty years have we understood its structure and function.[1] The first-century disciples never heard of DNA, but they lived out Christ's spiritual genetic code.

The technology of the twenty-first century promises virtual reality, but if it is not combined with first-century face-to-face reality, it produces disembodied holograms. Today's communications revolution is intersecting with a Bible-storying revolution that is launching a discipleship revolution in the twenty-first century.

The following diagram broadens the course map on page 19 to a DNA21 strategy. By putting Bible storying together with making disciples in small groups, we have a strategy that can transform the church and turn the world upside down.

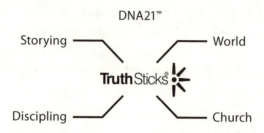

We stand at a crossroads for Christians, families, small groups, churches, and our nation. We need a revolution that reestablishes first-century disciple making as Jesus practiced and commanded. Where do you find yourself in the following dialogue?

We're starting a revolution! Wanna come along?

You are starting a revolution?

Well, we aren't starting it; Jesus did. We are just fanning the flames. Praise God that in some places the revolution has already begun. Will you join us?

Okay, you've got my attention. What do you mean by revolution?

Jesus started the discipleship revolution when He said: "If anyone would come after me, he must deny himself and take up his cross daily and follow me" (Luke 9:23).

That sounds hard.

Somewhere along the way people tried to domesticate the revolution. Sometimes they were able to tame it. After all, revolutions can be dangerous.

I hear you, brother. But, say, I'm not really into that whole danger thing.

Do you want to come along or not? Revolutions are not for sissies! Revolutions change things.

I'm no sissy, but I don't like change. I'm comfortable with my daily to-do list.

Revolutions change things and take time.

Hey, but I don't have an extra minute in my schedule. Can you just shrink that revolution thing a bit so that it fits my timetable?

Revolutions include demonstrations.

Well, I don't want to force my opinions on anyone. Let's make it a chat room where people opt in. If I stick my neck out, it could get chopped off.

Revolutions are costly.

Have you seen my credit report? We lost most of our savings in the economic downturn. Don't you read the headlines? We're trying to keep what we have.

Revolutions change everything.

That's radical. My comfort zone is pretty small these days.

Jesus came saying, "The time has come. . . . The kingdom of God is near. Repent and believe the good news!" (Mark 1:15).

Repentance means changing everything, doesn't it?

Yep.

Okay . . . I'm not backing away just yet. What does He want us to do?

The kingdom of God is near. Get ready. The King is coming. Fill in the potholes. Repair the bridges. Straighten out the curves. Make an interstate. The King is coming!

That sounds exciting.

He is calling for you to see His glory, tell His story, and make disciples of all peoples. It's time to do a U-turn.

Is that repentance?

You got it! Jesus is sparking a discipleship revolution in the twenty-first century that changes everything, like the one He started in the first century.

Count me in. Where do I enlist?[2]

At the foot of the cross!

Wait a minute. I am talking to you — the reader. We have come a long way on our journey through this book. You understand the changes necessary to join us. Wanna come along?

What do I do next?

Make disciples as Jesus did. Tell Bible stories. Start a discipleship revolution in your sphere of influence.

How do I do that?

Make truth stick. Get the Word into people's lives and on their lips. "Now that you know these things, God will bless you for doing them" (John 13:17, NLT).

WHY THE JOHNNYS OF AMERICA CAN'T, DON'T, OR WON'T READ

Rudolf Flesch wrote a best-seller in 1955 titled *Why Johnny Can't Read and What You Can Do About It.* This landmark book could be mistaken as a frustrated teacher's attempt to demonize television's impact on reading and make a case for phonetics. However, it raised a national debate about literacy's decline in America. One man named Theodor S. Geisel took up the challenge to increase literacy levels among children. We all know him by his pen name—Dr. Seuss—and in 1957 he published *The Cat in the Hat* and *How the Grinch Stole Christmas!*[1]

About half of Americans prefer an oral approach to communicating and learning. While 25 to 33 percent of the world is truly illiterate, only 4 to 5 percent of Americans have not been to school. That has lulled us into overlooking the statistics that show more than one out of two Americans and two out of three of the world's population do not read proficiently enough for daily living.

In 2003, the U.S. Department of Education divided literacy into four groupings: *below basic, basic, intermediate,* and *proficient.* (These terms replace the terms *illiterate* and *functionally illiterate*, which were used in the 1992 survey.)

1. Below Basic—14 percent (one in seven)
   - Signs name, finds medicine dosage
2. Basic—36 percent
   - Compares ticket prices; reads pamphlet

3. Intermediate—37 percent
   ▪ Reads novels and for leisure
   ▪ Scans the Internet for information
   ▪ Connects through social media, such as Facebook
   ▪ Reads maps and charts, such as checkbook, when required
4. Proficient—13 percent
   ▪ Finds, maintains, and uses information from continuous paragraphs
   ▪ Only one-third of all college graduates[2]

The 2003 National Assessment of Adult Literacy (NAAL) surveyed 18,500 people in their homes or in prisons. NAAL estimates that one in seven adults (about 30 million people) fall in the "below basic" category for handling basic prose in English (like in the Bible).

Similar to what the Department of Education reported in 1992, the 2003 interviews confirmed that about half of all U.S. adults (about 93 million people) fall into the "below basic" or "basic" reading categories. Although there were more college graduates in 1992 than in 2003, fewer were reading at the proficient level, falling from 40 percent in 1992 to 31 percent in 2003. In the following diagram "How People Learn and the Use of Exposition: A Learning Grid," Mark Snowden has updated a chart developed by Jim Slack and D. P. Smith. It depicts the amount of literate worldview exposition of biblical text that can be included in the biblical narrative and the post-story dialogue session. This chart matches the learning levels of the most recent NAAL research.

	Oral Communicator Below Basic	Oral Communicator Basic	Oral Literate Communicator Intermediate	Literate Communicator Proficient	
Story	No Exposition	Some Exposition	Story with Exposition or Exposition	No Story or Story with as Much Exposition as Needed	Story
Exposition					
Dialog	No Exposition	Moderate Exposition	Exposition in Dialog	As Much Exposition as Desired or Interest Calls for	Dialog

Joe: "Below Basic" Reading Level[3]

Joe is a waste-management worker in Seattle. He and his wife, Mary, have two boys and a girl. Joe never went to school. Although he is surrounded by writing and knows that letters and words exist, he doesn't think of words as concrete "things." To Joe, words are simply the sounds he uses to paint oral pictures on his listener's mental canvas. He doesn't spend time thinking abstractly about words or their definitions because their meanings depend on the context.

Joe cannot read or write. He doesn't recognize written words; he just sees them as squiggles. Words have no exact meeting to Joe, so any word analysis is lost on him. To him, words are sounds or pictures, not objects. Joe learns through stories, proverbs, songs, and practical experience. He concentrates on what he can see and has experienced. And Joe is not alone. One in seven of the U.S. population is an oral communicator like Joe.

Joe sticks to a routine, seldom travels, and entertains his children with funny stories from his day at work. But as soon as he finishes speaking, the story "disappears." It is gone forever unless he repeats it. So the children beg him, "Tell it again!" and they repeat it to their friends the next day. Mary listens, too, so she has something new to tell her neighbor when they meet in the park.

Steve: "Basic" Reading Level

Steve has worked in retail sales since dropping out just before his freshman year of high school. Steve will tell you he can read, but it's been years since he's picked up a book, newspaper, or magazine. He listens to news radio on the way to work and catches trends from his customers or those with whom he works.

Steve currently sells clothes in a department store at the mall and has set monthly sales records with his outgoing personality. He can read the clothing tags, handle the computerized cash register, and manage the inventory lists. It takes energy, but he copes.

Once when Steve had the guys and their lady friends over, he bought a popular book on sale at the front of the store and left it on a coffee table to impress them. His friends never discuss books—although they do discuss the latest movies or sports—so he's rarely put on the spot.

In the United States, Steve and those like him comprise one out of every three people (36 percent). Steve is considered to be literate by every country in the world. However, Steve's values are not shaped by what he reads but by the people he meets and media sources he trusts. Although Steve started out in school reading and writing, he is clearly an oral communicator.

Marsha: "Intermediate" Reading Level

Steve's wife, Marsha, is thirty. She grew up in Boise, where she graduated from high school. After she married Steve, she worked in a bank until her first child was born, but since then she's been a housewife. She wrote letters to her mother every week when she was first married.

Marsha likes to read. Mostly, she reads novels that she swaps with girlfriends or checks out from the public library. But her favorite entertainment is *Desperate Housewives* on TV. Marsha helps her daughter with her sixth-grade schoolwork and sees that all the assignments are done on time. When Marsha needs information for herself, she may scan Internet sites, but she prefers to find someone to tell her or show her. In spite of her education, she still thinks of people as being the best sources of information. She may understand explanations that use points, lists, tables, or steps—it depends on the subject—but she has a hard time remembering them long enough to tell someone else.

Marsha is like one-third of all Americans (37 percent) who fall in the gray zone between oral and literate communicators. It depends upon the topic, energy required, and time she has available. However, over time, she actually learns faster, deeper, and then retains information longer through oral means.

Brian and Lindsay: "Proficient" Reading Level

Brian is a twenty-two-year-old history major at Georgia Tech. Unlike most of his classmates, he enjoys the reading assignments and reads extra material not required for his classes. He and fiancée Lindsay, who is an economics major, do schoolwork on their computers. Brian uses the Internet, Facebook, and Twitter to communicate with his friends, do research for his classes, and surf the Web. Brian does not expect repetition in the classroom, and he enjoys getting new information each time. He and Lindsay both prefer reading material that is arranged like a Web page with pictures and textboxes. They groan at the sight of books with long chapters or long paragraphs and not enough illustrations!

As print communicators, Brian and Lindsay are able to learn and share information using teaching points, outlines, lists, tables, graphs, and steps in a plan. But they are always ready to enjoy a good story, and they have their favorite songs loaded on their MP3 players and catch online TV programs they always seem to miss. Even for them, practical experience or apprenticeship is absolutely essential for changing their values and behavior and being able to pass those values on to others. They represent the 18 to 20 percent who are highly literate.

FACTORING IN READING REGRESSION

Determining a reading level is not as easy as it sounds. Jim Slack, a storying pioneer, has pointed out that people who profess to be readers in a culture must read on a regular basis to maintain their comprehension skills.

Reading abilities decline as nonprint sources provide information that was once available only through printed means. Further, unless a student achieves at least a ninth-grade level of reading—or, more accurately, has been reading for at least nine years—it is easy to suspect an oral learning preference or anticipate that if education is discontinued, the student will slide back into an oral-preference world.

Jim also said, "Unless students have books to use in the classroom and books that are available to take home for reading in their spare time, the student, even if reaching the ninth grade, will probably still remain an oral learner."[4]

The use of Chronological Bible Storying, TruthSticks, and other oral methodologies are certainly affected by, but not limited to, a person's literacy level. People who have an oral learning preference and a desire to make disciples can use both oral and literate means to influence those in America who can't, won't, or don't read.

GLOSSARY

The following terms are defined as they are used in this book.

barrier: The aspects of culture, circumstances, or religion that hinder a listener in hearing, understanding, or acting upon the message of the gospel. These are the stumbling blocks. Barriers are discerned by studying the worldview. Barriers are beliefs, practices, or experiences that might keep unbelievers from understanding or accepting spiritual truths. Prior experiences, such as with nominal Christians, may also pose barriers. See **bridges**.

basic level reader: A person who has attained a reading proficiency that enables him or her to read basic materials, such as comparing ticket prices and reading a brochure for jury duty. Considered an oral learner. Thirty-six percent of all Americans fall into this category.

below-basic level reader: A person who has only the simplest reading skills, such as signing one's name or reading medicine dosage. Considered an oral learner. Fourteen percent of all Americans (one in seven) are at this level, including 4 to 5 percent who cannot read at all.

Bible storying: See **storying**.

Bible truths: What the Bible teaches as truth; those biblical truths that are the foundation or essence of truth leading to salvation, the New Testament church, the discipled life, and

Christian leadership. The three terms *essential Bible truths*, *basic Bible truths*, and *universal Bible truths* all describe the generic or basic biblical truths.

biblical illiteracy: A condition or state resulting from little or no knowledge of the Bible, its message, or how to apply its truths. Frequently exhibited by people who confuse Bible facts or who answer questions with secular wisdom and attribute it to sacred writ. This ignorance can result in a person developing his or her own theology or beliefs.

biblical worldview: Believing that absolute moral truth exists and that the Bible is totally accurate in all it teaches, realizing that what the Bible teaches is the real perspective on the world for Christians, and following it in life. Barna uses the term to describe eight biblical truths that are accepted by conservative Christians.

branching: The intentional act of beginning a new small group out of an existing small group. May involve a period of transition during which the group leader trains an apprentice who will leave the small group, possibly with a few others from the group, to start a new group.

bridges: The beliefs, practices, or experiences of a culture that can have a beneficial influence upon a person's consideration of the gospel. They include God-given opportunities for witness in which needs felt within the culture are met by the Christian faith. Bridges are discerned by studying the worldview and can provide openings for heightened interest and greater relevance of the biblical message to a person's worldview. The storyer can intentionally target issues deemed significant to the listener. See **barriers**.

Christian: Anyone who professes (self-identifies) to be a Christian, on either a church-membership roll, a public-opinion poll, or a government census. This term embraces all traditions and confessions and is not an indicator of the degree of commitment or theological orthodoxy.

Chronological Bible Storying: A method of sharing biblical truths by telling the stories of the Bible as intact stories in the order that they happened in time. The person using this method leads the hearers to discover the truths in the stories for the purpose of evangelization, discipleship, church planting, and leader training. Jim Slack and J. O. Terry developed Chronological Bible Storying when they saw the need for a purely oral approach to oral peoples. They coined the term *storying* to differentiate Chronological Bible Storying from Chronological Bible Teaching.

communication preference: The favorite style or method of communication for an individual or group of people. There are two dominant poles in a communication-preference continuum—oral and literate—and numerous combinations in between. There are major differences between literate or print-oriented communicators and oral communicators in the way they receive information.

contextualization of the gospel: Presentation of the gospel message and Christian beliefs that effectively addresses bridges, barriers, and gaps within the worldview of a people group or population segment.

culture: The unique customs, skills, arts, language, and other interrelated learned behavior patterns of a people that shape how they think, perceive, feel, and interact with the world around them. These patterns set them apart as a distinct group or society.

dialogue: The discussion following the told Bible story devoted to understanding and applying the biblical narrative. It is built around questions and answers by the leader and the participants and involves discussion of the story, drawing out God's truths, and developing life applications.

disciple: A person who has a personal obedient, growing relationship as a follower of Jesus Christ.

discipleship: The Christian's commitment to the person, teaching, and Spirit of Jesus Christ involving progressive learning, growth in Christlikeness, application of biblical truth, and taking responsibility for teaching others to do the same.

evangelical: A Christian who believes that Jesus Christ is the sole source of salvation through faith in Him, has personal faith resulting in regeneration by the Holy Spirit, recognizes the inspired Word of God as the only basis for faith and Christian living, and is committed to biblical preaching and evangelism that brings others to faith in Jesus Christ. Some churches that are not considered evangelical in faith and practice may contain members who are evangelicals.

evangelism: The sharing of the good news of the gospel; God's act of working through believers, empowered by the Holy Spirit, to communicate the good news (gospel) of Jesus Christ to every person and people group. The gospel should be communicated with sufficient cultural and personal relevance for a person to respond to Christ by faith (conversion) or to reject Him.

experiential learning: Educational term for the process of actively engaging students in an authentic experience with expected benefits and consequences. Students make discoveries and experiment with knowledge themselves instead of hearing or reading about the experiences of others. Students also reflect on their experiences, thus developing new skills, new attitudes, and new theories or ways of thinking. The student is usually involved in his or her learning to a much greater degree than in traditional learning environments. Related terms and concepts include active learning, hands-on learning, deep-level processing, and higher-order thinking.

gaps: Areas where one's worldview does not have a corresponding concept in accord with the biblical worldview; neither a worldview bridge nor barrier.

intermediate level reader: A person who can handle basic prose and continuous text found in articles and books. Considered a literate but can have a nonreading (oral) learning preference. Thirty-seven percent of all Americans.

learning preference (style): Distinctively different ways students learn, such as emphasis on oral or visual activities.

missions: The whole enterprise of sending and going to share the gospel cross-culturally as an expression of commitment to God's redemptive purpose. Cross-cultural opportunities that believers are afforded and seize that give them a platform for carrying out God's will for evangelism, church planting, discipleship, and leader training.

obedience-based discipleship: The immediate response of doing what Christ and the Bible commands. This pattern is learned and practiced through the process of following Jesus Christ as Lord without reservation.

oral Bible: The accumulated Bible stories that are told to an oral society, typically between 25 and 225 stories. These are usually told in chronological order, though not always, since many times specific problems, concerns, and fears may need to be addressed first. The stories chosen may differ from one culture to another, depending on felt/actual needs, worldview, and theology. Those stories that form the cornerstone of Christian faith will be represented in all oral Bible collections. An accumulation of Bible stories that have been storied to oral communicators or that can be recalled by memory enables them to meditate upon God's Word in their quiet times and devotionals and use the stories in evangelism, discipleship, church planting, and leadership development—and often going where the written Bible cannot go.

orality: Reliance on spoken rather than written language for communication. The mutually reinforcing combination of cognitive, communicational, and relational characteristics that result when a culture relies on spoken language for communication. The quality or state of being oral.

oral-preference learner: Someone who prefers to learn or process information by oral rather than written means. (Thus, it includes literate people whose preferred communication style is oral rather than literate, even though they can read.) Also, someone who cannot read or write. Someone whose favorite or most effective communication and learning format, style, or method is in accordance with oral formats, as contrasted with literate formats.

proficient level reader: A person who can find, maintain, and use information from continuous prose found in articles and books. Literate, but may still display a nonreading (oral) learning preference. Thirteen percent of all Americans. Only one-third of college graduates are proficient readers.

reproducibility: (1) Duplicating a small-group leader's basic ministry and lifestyle in the lives of others to the point that they can lead others to become like and serve like the person.
(2) Ministries, groups, patterns, and resources that can be continued locally without external contributions required to keep them sustained or ongoing.

scriptural authority: The supreme standard of truth is the Bible by which all human conduct, creeds, and religious opinions should be tried.

secularization: A process of decline in the influence of religion on society.

small group: The meeting of believers for the purpose of spiritual maturation. May be open to anyone, including nonbelievers, or closed to outsiders. Location of the meeting may be anywhere the group chooses to meet, ranging from living rooms in homes to church classrooms or break rooms at work. May be called by different names, including home group.

small-group leader: A believer who is responsible for facilitating a small group. It is assumed that the leader plays a key role in the spiritual growth of the group and each participant's spiritual-growth process and will provide Scripture, facilitate interaction, and handle follow-up as needed.

spiritual growth: Personal maturation in faith and practice that encompasses knowledge, character, and skill development. Often depicted as family life stages including infant, child, young adult, parent, and grandparent.

story set: A collection of stories that uses biblical truths to address a number of worldview-specific barriers to faith and practice; it also reinforces good things that form a bridge to understanding and obedience. These sets may be chronological or thematic depending on the needs of the learners.

storying/Bible storying: A narrative presentation designed to communicate a Bible story to oral-preference communicators; ideally it includes dialogue, interpretation, application, and accountability. It may also include drama, songs, poetry, and proverbs depicting the story.

Teflon: A coating material to which other substances have trouble clinging; this material is resistant to corrosive chemicals.

TruthSticks: The process of using Bible storying in relational small groups that intentionally makes disciples who continue the reproductive process in others.

Velcro: A fastening system of tiny plastic hooks and loops, named for a combination of two French words, *velour* (velvet) and *crochet* (hook).

worldview: Sum total of a people group's understanding of its world, including beliefs, values, and shared perceptions of reality. The way a specific people view the world around them. Members of a culture look *through* their worldview, not *at* it—somewhat like wearing tinted lenses. It is seldom apparent to its adherents unless it comes under question; it consists of fundamental cognitive, affective, and evaluative assumptions about reality. It forms the core of a culture, which guides people in how to act, think, believe, function, and relate. It can also be a profile of the way people within a specified culture live, act, think, work, and relate.

RECOMMENDED RESOURCES

The following three families of resources are sequential, but you may enter through any of the multiple opportunities offered and move to the others as they intersect personal needs or church schedules.

LEARNING TO SOAR FAMILY — INTRODUCES DISCIPLESHIP AND BIBLE STORYING

Learning to Soar: How to Grow Through Transitions and Trials by Avery T. Willis Jr. and Matt Willis (NavPress, 2009) — This book appeals to people regardless of their spiritual-growth level because of their felt needs and introduces them to discipleship and Bible storying. The small-group guide in the back of the book introduces the readers to the need to grow as disciples and to learn to tell Bible stories in each of the eight sessions.

Learning to Soar by Peter Roberts — This video portrays each of the four stages of the eagle's development (from the nest to soaring) in two- to three-minute chapters. Ideal for use by pastors who preach on the Bible stories for eight weeks or for use in small groups. Available from www.learningtosoar.org.

www.learningtosoar.org — This interactive website provides video training in Bible storying, videos that go with the chapters, and other resources, including opportunities for participants to share with others their continuing experiences at each of the four stages on this journey. Participants are encouraged to post songs, dramas, poems, and testimonies.

TRUTH THAT STICKS FAMILY — SHOWS HOW TO MAKE DISCIPLES USING BIBLE STORYING

Truth That Sticks: Communicating Velcro Truth in a Teflon World by Avery T. Willis Jr. and Mark Snowden (NavPress, 2010)

www.truthsticks.com — This website includes online resources and perspectives of storying and discipleship.

www.dna-21.org — This website provides many resources to use in a discipleship revolution.

REAL LIFE MINISTRIES — DEVELOPING A DISCIPLE-MAKING CHURCH

Real-Life Discipleship: Building Churches That Make Disciples by Jim Putman (NavPress, 2010) — This book is for pastors and church leaders. It shows how a church can become a disciple-making church.

Real-Life Discipleship Training Manual: Equipping Disciples Who Make Disciples by Jim Putman, Avery T. Willis Jr., Bill Krause, and Brandon Guindon (NavPress, 2010) — This twelve-week interactive manual trains and equips small-group leaders to disciple members using Bible stories.

Following Jesus Together (NavPress, 2010) — This five-CD set includes thirty-four audio stories of Jesus interacting with His disciples, covering the Gospels and Acts. It includes additional questions to use in small groups.

OTHER DISCIPLESHIP RESOURCES

DESIGN FOR DISCIPLESHIP Series
Learn more about the wealth that is available to you in Jesus Christ through the DESIGN FOR DISCIPLESHIP (DFD) Bible-study series. On your own or with a group, discover what it means to be a Christ-centered disciple, how to develop Christian character, how to have victory over sin, and how to grow toward maturity in your daily walk with God. Available from NavPress.com.

- Your Life in Christ
- The Spirit-Filled Christian
- Walking with Christ
- The Character of the Christian
- Foundations for Faith
- Growing in Discipleship
- Our Hope in Christ

2:7 Series
These studies are invaluable discipleship tools for those seeking to strengthen quiet times, equip for evangelism, deepen their relationship with God, and hide His Word in their hearts. They include Scripture memory designed to help with personal spiritual transformation. Available from NavPress.com.

- Growing Strong in God's Family
- Deepening Your Roots in God's Family
- Bearing Fruit in God's Family

LIFECHANGE Series
The LIFECHANGE Bible-study series can help you grow in Christlikeness through a life-changing encounter with God's Word. Discover what

the Bible says—not what someone else thinks it says—and develop the skills and desire to dig even deeper into God's Word. Each study includes study aids and discussion questions. Available from NavPress .com.

- James
- Proverbs
- Romans
- Acts
- And many more books of the Bible

MasterLife
MasterLife: A Biblical Process for Growing Disciples by Avery T. Willis Jr. with Kay Moore (LifeWay, 1996)—If God has spoken to you about becoming a more mature disciple, the *MasterLife* discipleship process will enable you to master life by making Christ the Master of your life. God has used this process in the lives of hundreds of thousands of literate learners all around the world to develop a personal, lifelong obedient relationship with Jesus in which He transforms their character into Christlikeness, changes their values into kingdom values, and involves them in His mission in the home, the church, and the world. It consists of the following books:

- *MasterLife 1: The Disciple's Cross* explains step-by-step how to practice the six biblical disciplines of an obedient disciple.
- *MasterLife 2: The Disciple's Personality* shows how to live in the Spirit and become more like Christ.
- *MasterLife 3: The Disciple's Victory* reveals the secret for the disciple to triumph over the world, the flesh, and the Devil.
- *MasterLife 4: The Disciple's Mission* helps the disciple identify his or her own stage of growth and role in discipling others.
- *The MasterLife Book Set* contains all four MasterLife Member Books above (six 6-week sessions each) in a slipcase at a savings.

- *The MasterLife Leader's Kit* provides step-by-step instructions for facilitating small-group discipleship studies and three DVDs to prepare the leader and for use in the small group at appropriate places.
- *MasterLife: Developing a Rich Personal Relationship with the Master* by Avery T. Willis Jr. and Sherrie Willis Brown (B & H, 1998) — This is a paperback book of the content without the discipleship process. It gives the leader or small-group member an overview of the *MasterLife* content but is not a substitute for the small-group discipling process.

ORALITY RESOURCES

Websites
- www.finishingthetask.com — for evangelism, discipleship, and church planting among unreached people groups
- www.reallifeministries.com — in the United States
- www.echothestory.com — with youth
- www.chronologicalbiblestorying.com and www.oralstrategies .org — for Bible storying

Books
- *Story Thru the Bible* (NavPress, March 2011) is a resource that provides fifty-two story guides from the Old and New Testaments to be used by small groups to tell God's story and discuss the implications for everyday life.
- *Making Disciples of Oral Learners* by the Lausanne Group: Download the book for free at www.internationaloralitynet-work.com or purchase it at www.imbresources.org. Available in English, Chinese traditional and simplified script, Korean, Arabic, and Spanish.
- Interactive course: *Tell the Story*, an International Centre for

Excellence in Leadership (ICEL) primer on Chronological Bible Storying available from www.imbresources.org.

- *The Art of Storytelling* by John Walsh (Chicago: Moody Press, 2003).
- *Basic Bible Storying* by J. O. Terry (Fort Worth, TX: Church Starting Network, 2007).
- *Shaped by the Story* by Michael Novelli (Grand Rapids, MI: Zondervan, 2008).

Videos

These are both available from www.imbresources.org.

- *Telling the Story*—Introduction to orality with examples.
- *Orality Around the World* DVD—Fourteen vignettes of storying around the world.

This list is intended to be brief. There are many more good resources available on the wbsites listed.

ORALITY MINISTRIES

- www.averywillis.org
- www.OneStory.org
- www.go2SouthAsia.org
- www.gods-story.org/bibleatlast.htm
- www.siutraining.org
- www.StoryRunners.com

MISSIONS

The Biblical Basis of Missions: Your Mission as a Christian by Avery T. Willis Jr. (Convention Press, 1979) is only available by

download at www.averywillis.org or www.imb.org/main/
biblicalbasis.asp?StoryID=8080&LanguageID=1709.
On Mission with God: Living God's Purpose for His Glory by Avery T.
Willis Jr. and Henry T. Blackaby (LifeWay, 2001) is a natural follow-up for *Experiencing God* by Henry Blackaby and
MasterLife by Avery Willis. It uses the stories of the Bible's
seven key characters (Abraham, Moses, David, Jesus, Peter,
Paul, and John) to show how God involves us in His mission
for His glory. The following resources are for use in an eight-
week small group study.

- *On Mission with God* Workbook
- *On Mission with God* Leader's Kit with videos for
  each session
- *On Mission with God* hardcover book
- *On Mission with God*, a module of nine audio
  CDs telling eighty-eight Bible stories from the
  lives of the seven characters featured in the books
  above, plus Sarah and Mary. It is Module 7 in the
  Following Jesus: Making Disciples of Oral Learners
  series by Avery T. Willis Jr. Available from www
  .learningtosoar.org, www.imb.org, and www
  .fjseries.org.

ORGANIZATIONS

*Avery T. Willis Center for Global Outreach at Oklahoma Baptist
University,* Shawnee, Oklahoma, provides a major in orality
and is seeking accreditation for a master of arts degree with
an emphasis in orality that can be pursued online. OBU
equips students for vocational Christian service any place on
the globe, provides missiological research tools for students
engaged in the study of missions, and prepares them for

short-term volunteer assignments. It helps students, faculty, and staff to develop and live out a missions lifestyle through hosting missions conferences, developing missions education resources, and coordinating short-term opportunities for missions service in our nation and throughout the world.

Call2All is a worldwide strategy-centered and action-oriented movement calling the church to a renewed, focused, collaborative effort to complete the Great Commission. It convenes Christian leaders in strategy congresses and provides new avenues for training in comprehensive strategies in orality, church planting, evangelism, prayer, unreached people groups, and geographical mapping to reach the last, the least, and the lost. www.Call2All.org

Finishing the Task is a global network of local churches, denominations, church planters, and missions agencies that are working together in partnership to see church-planting initiatives launched initially among the 639 unengaged, unreached people groups of the world with populations over 100,000 — and eventually all people groups. www.finishingthetask.com

International Orality Network is a network of more than one hundred organizations making God's Word available to oral learners in culturally appropriate ways that enable church-planting movements everywhere. www.internationaloralitynetwork .com

Lausanne Committee for World Evangelism is a worldwide movement that mobilizes evangelical leaders to collaborate for world evangelism. www.lausanne.org

OneStory works with mother-tongue speakers to develop and record worldview-sensitive, chronological "Bible story sets" for each specific group — typically twenty-five to sixty stories in a two-year period. Mother-tongue speakers spread the stories to others. These story sets form the beginnings of an "oral Bible" to be told and retold for generations. www.OneStory.org

Trans World Radio has more than two thousand radio stations broadcasting in more than two hundred languages. www.twr.org

NOTES

Introduction

1. "Test Your Awareness: Do the Test," public relations commercial released by Transport for London, http://www.dothetest.co.uk/basketball.html (accessed October 30, 2009).

2. Mark Kutner, Elizabeth Greenberg, and Justin Baer, "A First Look at the Literacy of America's Adults in the 21st Century," National Assessment of Adult Literacy, U.S. Department of Education, December 2005, 1–4, 15. Available online at http://nces.ed.gov/naal/pdf/2006470_1.pdf (accessed January 21, 2009).

3. See Lausanne Group, *Making Disciples of Oral Learners* (New York: Elim Printing, 2005).

Chapter 1: Communicating Velcro Truth in a Teflon World

1. According to http://www.velcro.com, the brand name Velcro is a fastening technology of hooks and loops that owns some 160 patents in the United States alone.

2. "Teflon," http://www.uselessinformation.org/teflon/index.html (accessed May 4, 2009).

3. Karl Fisch, Scott McLeod, Jeff Brenman, "Did You Know 3.0," available at http://www.youtube.com/watch?v=jpEnFwiqdx8&feature=related# (accessed October 30, 2009).

4. Fisch, McLeod, Brenman.

5. Cathy Lynn Grossman, "Americans get an 'F' in religion," *USA Today*, March 14, 2007, http://www.usatoday.com/news/religion/2007-03-07 -teaching-religion-cover_N.htm (accessed June 23, 2009).

6. Barna Group, "Most American Christians Do Not Believe that Satan or

the Holy Spirit Exist," April 10, 2009, http://www.barna.org/barna
-update/article/12-faithspirituality/260-most-american-christians-do-not
-believe-that-satan-or-the-holy-spirit-exis (accessed June 23, 2009).

7. Barna Group, "Christianity Is No Longer Americans' Default Faith,"
   January 12, 2009, http://www.barna.org/barna-update/article/12
   -faithspirituality/15-christianity-is-no-longer-americans-default-faith
   (accessed June 23, 2009).

8. Mark Kutner, Elizabeth Greenberg, and Justin Baer, "A First Look at the
   Literacy of America's Adults in the 21st Century," National Assessment of
   Adult Literacy, U.S. Department of Education, December 2005, 1–4, 15.
   Available online at http://nces.ed.gov/naal/pdf/2006470_1.pdf (accessed
   January 21, 2009).

9. Sally Gifford, "Literary Reading in Dramatic Decline, According to
   National Endowment for the Arts Survey," National Endowment for the
   Arts, July 8, 2004, http://www.nea.gov/news/news04/ReadingAtRisk.
   Html (accessed May 30, 2009).

10. Gifford.

11. Results of the first tests since 1992 are available in the publication "A First
    Look at the Literacy of America's Adults in the 21st Century." Available
    online at http://nces.ed.gov/naal/pdf/2006470_1.pdf. Grant Lovejoy has
    posted a more complete discussion of the results of the 2003 survey of
    18,500 people at http://www.chronologicalbiblestorying.com.

12. Dan Poynter, Book Industry Statistics, March 1, 2008, http://www
    .parapublishing.com/sites/para/resources/statistics.cfm (accessed
    December 19, 2009).

CHAPTER 2: WIRED FOR STORIES

1. *EE-Taow!* video (Sanford, FL: New Tribes Mission, 1989), excerpted from
   On Mission with God video (Nashville: LifeWay, 2002).

2. Information about the FOLLOWING JESUS series is online at http://www
   .fjseries.org. The seven modules are available from the International
   Mission Board at http://www.imbresources.org.

3. Stephen Stringer, interview by Avery Willis, June 11, 2009.

4. Michael Novelli, e-mail correspondence with Mark Snowden, August 4,
   2004.

5. PC Study Bible (Seattle: Biblesoft, 1992–2005).

6. Chip Heath and Dan Heath, *Made to Stick* (New York: Random House,
   2007), 16–17.

Chapter 3: Using the Sensory Gates

1. *Iraq—To the Ends of the Earth* video (Richmond, VA: International Mission Board, February 2004).
2. Samuel Chiang, e-mail correspondence with Avery Willis, July 28, 2009.
3. John Walsh, phone interview by Mark Snowden, September 26, 2009.
4. Walsh interview.

Chapter 4: Making the Bible Come to Life

1. Avery heard this at the OneStory commissioning service in Chiang Mai, Thailand, September 30, 2004.
2. You can listen to Lone Ranger radio programs online at http://www.lonerangerfanclub.com/lonerangerradio.html.
3. Jim Harris, interview by Avery Willis, March 26, 2007.
4. This is an element of Steve's speech to Campus Crusade for Christ International conferences and leaders; Avery has heard him say it many times.

Chapter 5: Head, Heart, Hands

1. Dennis Stokes and Ralph Ennis (The Navigators), interview by the authors, July 21, 2009.
2. Adapted from Don Falkos, 6218 Countryside Lane, Madison, WI, 53705, © 2008. Used by permission.
3. Stokes and Ennis interview.
4. For a practical guide for interpretation, see Principles of Interpretation that I included in the *Disciple's Study Bible*, Life Helps (Nashville: Holman Bible Publishers, 1988), 1769–1772.
5. Stokes and Ennis interview.
6. For more on DiSC, see http://www.onlinediscprofile.com.

Chapter 6: Face-to-Face

1. Jim Putman, *Church Is a Team Sport* (Grand Rapids, MI: Baker, 2008), 33.
2. Jim Blazin (home-groups pastor of Real Life Ministries), interview by Avery Willis, March 2007.
3. Avery Willis and Real Life Ministries staff, *Following Jesus Together* (Colorado Springs, CO: NavPress, 2010). Available at http://www.navpress.com.

4. Jim Harris and Brandon Guindon, interviews conducted and compiled by Mark Snowden, June 12, 2009, Post Falls, ID. Listen to an interview with Brandon online at http://www.reallifeministries.com/oldstories&q=avery%20willis.
5. Jim Blazin, interview by Mark Snowden, June 7, 2009, Post Falls, ID.
6. Todd Winslow, e-mail correspondence with Mark Snowden, June 18, 2009.
7. Richard Baker, interview by Mark Snowden, May 23, 2009.

CHAPTER 7: TOUCHED TO THE CORE

1. Daniel Pink, *A Whole New Mind* (New York: Berkley, 2005).
2. Claudia Kalb, "To Pluck a Rooted Sorrow," *Newsweek*, April 27, 2009.
3. Eric Jensen, *Teaching with the Brain in Mind* (Alexandria, VA: Association for Supervision and Curriculum Development, 1998), 75.
4. Mark Snowden's personal notes from John Walsh's training session at the International Orality Network annual workshop, October 2008, Dallas, TX.

CHAPTER 8: THE SWORD OF THE SPIRIT

1. George Barna, *Think Like Jesus* (Brentwood, TN: Integrity, 2003), 21.
2. Barna, 21.
3. Barna, 23.
4. "2009 Scripture Access Statistics," Wycliffe Bible Translators, November 2009, http://www.wycliffe.net/ScriptureAccessStatistics/tabid/73/language/en-US/Default.aspx (accessed January 21, 2010).
5. "2009 Scripture Access Statistics."
6. For a list of organizations that provide audio Bibles, see http://www.internationaloralitynetwork.com. In the left navigation is a list of resources.
7. Also, look on pages 69–70 for Don Falkos's method of asking questions that will help you remember the basic facts.
8. Dorothy Miller, interview by Avery Willis, September 12, 2005.
9. Benjamin Hawkins, "President's Classroom: Modeling Preaching Through Chapel," *SouthwesternNews* 67, no. 4 (Summer 2009), http://www.swbts.edu/swnews/articles_detail.cfm?Article_ID=250 (accessed July 28, 2009). Used by permission of the News and Information Office, Southwestern Baptist Theological Seminary, February 10, 2010.

CHAPTER 9: HOOKED FOR LIFE

1. Avery T. Willis Jr. and Kay Moore, *MasterLife* (Nashville: LifeWay, 1996), 8.
2. John Revell gave Avery Willis permission to share this story that he has written for a forthcoming book on making disciples, September 11, 2009.
3. Greg L. Hawkins and Cally Parkinson, *Reveal: Where Are You?* (South Barrington, IL: Willow Creek Resources, 2007), 4.
4. Ken Blanchard, Phil Hodges, Lee Ross, and Avery Willis, *Lead Like Jesus Study Guide* (Nashville: J. Countryman, 2003), 150.
5. Lisa Sells, interview by Avery Willis, August 6, 2009.

CHAPTER 10: JESUS' WAY OF MAKING TRUTH STICK

1. First reported by Avery T. Willis Jr., with Sherrie Willis Brown, *MasterLife: Developing a Rich Personal Relationship with the Master* (Nashville: B & H, 1998), 239.
2. Jim Putman, interview by Avery Willis, August 6, 2009.
3. Jim Blazin, interview by Mark Snowden, June 7, 2009, Post Falls, ID.

CHAPTER 11: THE SPIRITUAL-GROWTH STORY

1. See Avery T. Willis Jr. and Kay Moore, *MasterLife: A Biblical Process for Growing Disciples* (Nashville: LifeWay, 1997), 123; and Avery T. Willis Jr., *MasterBuilder: Multiplying Leaders* (Nashville: Baptist Sunday School Board, 1985), 16.
2. Statistics from the Global Research Department, International Mission Board, SBC.
3. This training is called Immersion I and Immersion II. See http://www.reallifeministries.com/association_home. The story is from an interview with Jim Putman by Avery Willis, August 6, 2009.
4. Ashley Hall, interview by Mark Snowden, May 23, 2009, Easley, SC.
5. Chad hall, interview by Mark Snowden, May 23, 2009, Easley, SC.
6. In his books *Church Is a Team Sport: A Championship Strategy for Doing Ministry Together* (Grand Rapids, MI: Baker, 2008) and *Real-Life Discipleship: Building Churches That Make Disciples* (Colorado Springs, CO: NavPress, 2010), Jim Putman explained in detail how to help leaders make disciples in a spiritual progression that ultimately reaches multiplication. For readers who have been discipled using *MasterLife*, I used a diagram of the spiritual-growth process called *MasterBuilder*. However,

I decided it was better to use what Real Life Ministries was familiar with here.

7. See Jim Putman, *Church Is a Team Sport* (Grand Rapids, MI: Baker, 2008), 146.

8. Jim Putman, interview by Avery Willis, August 6, 2009.

CHAPTER 12: A NEW OPERATING SYSTEM FOR WORLDVIEW

1. Roy Hewitt, "U.S. Shooter Matt Emmons Again Misses Gold on Final Shot Gaffe," *The Plain Dealer*, Cleveland.com, August 17, 2008, http://www.cleveland.com/olympics/index.ssf/2008/08/us_shooter_matt _emmons_again_m.html (accessed September 14, 2009).

2. Marc A. Fey, "Worldviews and Children," Focus on the Family, http://www.focusonthefamily.com/faith/christian_worldview/worldviews_and _children.aspx (accessed August 29, 2009).

3. Lloyd Kwast diagram used by permission; Ralph D. Winter, Steve C. Hawthorne, eds., *Perspectives on the World Christian Movement: A Reader* (Pasadena, CA: William Carey Library Publishers, 2009), 397–399. This version was adapted from the diagram used in *Making Disciples of Oral Learners* (Lausanne Committee for World Evangelization and International Orality Network, 2005), 36.

4. Tom Gilson, review of *unChristian*, by David Kinnaman, Thinking Christian blog, October 21, 2007, http://www.thinkingchristian.net/ C246305481/E20071021094207/index.html (accessed December 20, 2009).

5. "A New Generation Expresses Its Skepticism and Frustration with Christianity," The Barna Group, September 24, 2007, http://www .barna.org/barna-update/article/16-teensnext-gen/94-a-new-generation -expresses-its-skepticism-and-frustration-with-christianity (accessed September 2, 2009).

6. Barna, "A New Generation."

7. Barna, "A New Generation."

8. Barna, "A New Generation."

9. George Barna, *Think Like Jesus* (Brentwood, TN: Integrity, 2003), 20–22.

10. Humphrey Taylor, "Internet Users Now Spending an Average of 13 Hours a Week Online," Harris Interactive, December 23, 2009, http://www.b2i.us/profiles/investor/ResLibraryView.asp?ResLibraryID=35164& GoTopage=1&Category=1777&BzID=1963&t=11 (accessed February 10, 2010).

11. "College Students Spend 12 Hours/Day with Media, Gadgets," Alloy media+marketing, November 30, 2009, http://www.marketingcharts .com/television/college-students-spend-12-hoursday-with-media -gadgets-11195 (accessed February 10, 2010).
12. Ryan Bilsborrow-Koo, "Ten video sharing services compared," Digital Video Guru, April 7, 2006, http://www.dvguru.com/2006/04/07/ten -video-sharing-services-compared (accessed August 29, 2009).
13. N. T. Wright, "How Can the Bible Be Authoritative?" Laing Lecture 1989 and Griffith Thomas Lecture 1989. Originally published in *Vox Evangelica*, 1991, 21, 7–32, http://www.ntwrightpage.com/Wright _Bible_Authoritative.htm (accessed August 29, 2009).
14. Gilles Gravelle, phone interview by Mark Snowden, September 4, 2009. In a follow-up e-mail exchange with Mark, Gilles Gravelle credited the ice cream/insulin concept to Stand To Reason (http://www.str.org).
15. For further reading on worldview development, we recommend chapter 4 in *Making Disciples of Oral Learners* and module 1 of the *Following Jesus* audio series listed in the resource section of this book.
16. Malcom Gladwell, *Outliers: The Story of Success* (New York: Little, Brown, 2008), 166–170.
17. Caesar Kalinowski, interview by Mark Snowden, May 21, 2009.
18. Kalinowski interview.

CHAPTER 13: PASSING IT ON

1. Randy Proctor, e-mail correspondence with Mark Snowden, August 14, 2009.
2. Ed Stetzer, "Counting People Who Attend House Churches," The LifeWay Research Blog, September 3, 2009, http://blogs.lifeway.com/ blog/edstetzer/2009/09/house-churches.html (accessed October 4, 2009).
3. David Roach, "Americans open to invitations to church," Baptist Press, March 27, 2009, http://www.bpnews.net/BPnews.asp?ID=30161 (accessed October 4, 2009).
4. Jim Harris (Real Life Ministries), story related to Avery Willis in early consultations, March 2006.
5. Jim Blazin, interview by Mark Snowden, June 7, 2009, Post Falls, ID.
6. George Barna, *Think Like Jesus* (Brentwood, TN: Integrity, 2003), 23.
7. *Story Thru the Bible* will be available from NavPress in March 2011.
8. A seven-panel cube that tells the story of the gospel in pictures.

CHAPTER 14: LASTING CHANGE

1. For a summary of the eight steps in Kotter's change process, see http://www.mindtools.com/pages/article/newPPM_82.htm.
2. First reported by Avery T. Willis Jr., with Sherrie Willis Brown, *MasterLife: Developing a Rich Personal Relationship with the Master* (Nashville: B & H, 1998), 22.
3. Jim and Janet Stahl, interview by Avery Willis, September 11, 2009.
4. See appendix for details.
5. Adapted from Jawaharlal Mariappan, Angela Shih, and Peter G. Schrader, "Use of Scenario-Based Learning Approach in Teaching Statics," session 2666 (Ponoma, CA: California State Polytechnic University, Pomona, 2004), 3. Proceedings of the 2004 American Society for Engineering Education Annual Conference and Exposition.
6. The Learning Pyramid has been called into question by some because although the NTL believes the numbers to be accurate, they can no longer trace the original research that provided the percentages. See http://www.learningandteaching.info/learning/myths.htm for more information (accessed January 4, 2010).
7. Jim Putman, interview by Avery Willis, August 6, 2009.
8. Brandon Guindon, e-mail correspondence with Mark Snowden, September 25, 2009.
9. *Following Jesus: Making Disciples of Oral Learners* (San Clemente, CA: Progressive Vision, 2005). The FOLLOWING JESUS series is available at http://www.fjseries.org.
10. Real Life Ministries Association provides two-day monthly training sessions, called Immersion I and Immersion II, for churches desiring to make the change to small-group discipling using Bible storying. Find more information at http://www.reallifeministries.com/association_home.

CHAPTER 15: MULTIPLYING

1. For more information on LCWE, visit their website: http://www.lausanne.org.
2. Steve Douglass, interview by Avery Willis and Mark Snowden, September 3, 2009.
3. Bob Buford, *Half Time: Changing Your Game Plan from Success to Significance* (Grand Rapids, MI: Zondervan, 2004), 1.
4. Gene Jacobs, interview by Mark Snowden, June 9, 2009, Post Falls, ID.
5. Paul Krueger, phone interview by Mark Snowden, July 2, 2009; and

Chuck Broughton, e-mail correspondence with Mark Snowden, July 2009.

6. Jim Putman, phone interview by Avery Willis, September 15, 2009.
7. Gene Jacobs (Real Life Ministries), interview by Mark Snowden, June 9, 2009, Post Falls, ID.
8. Jim Putman interview, *Following Jesus Together* audio CD (Post Falls, ID: Real Life Ministries and Avery Willis, 2007)
9. Jim Putman, *Church Is a Team Sport* (Grand Rapids, MI: Baker, 2008), 126, 154.
10. Jacobs interview.
11. Jacobs interview.
12. Jim Putman, interview by Mark Snowden, June 8, 2009, Post Falls, ID.
13. J. O. Terry has developed the Bible Storying Handbook for training missions volunteers to use storying in overseas missions trips. The manual is available by writing jot2@sbcglobal.net.
14. Story as told to Avery Willis by Maasai leaders.
15. Dorothy Miller, "The God's Story Project — India," report from God's Story Project received via e-mail, September 19, 2009.

EPILOGUE

1. "Putting DNA to Work," Marian Koshland Science Museum of the National Academy of Sciences, http://www.koshland-science-museum.org/exhibitdna (accessed July 10, 2009).
2. For more on the DNA21: Discipleship Revolution, see http://www.dna-21.org.

APPENDIX

1. "Why Johnny Can't Read," Encyclopedia.com, http://www.encyclopedia.com/doc/1G2-3468301854.html (accessed July 28, 2009).
2. Mark Kutner, Elizabeth Greenberg, and Justin Baer, "A First Look at the Literacy of America's Adults in the 21st Century," National Assessment of Adult Literacy, U.S. Department of Education, December 2005, 1–4, 15. Available online at http://nces.ed.gov/naal/pdf/2006470_1.pdf (accessed January 21, 2009).
3. Jim Slack and Mark Snowden, "Four Learning Styles," unpublished PowerPoint, used by permission, September 2009.
4. Mark Snowden's memory of the quote by Jim Slack from several training sessions they led together, the last being in Kathmandu, Nepal, November 2004.

ABOUT THE AUTHORS

AVERY T. WILLIS JR. is an international author, leader, speaker, and conference leader. Among other things, he serves as executive director of the International Orality Network and ambassador-at-large for the Avery T. Willis Center for Global Outreach at Oklahoma Baptist University.

He was a pastor for ten years before serving for fourteen years with his wife, Shirley, and their five children as missionaries in Indonesia. He may be best known for creating the *MasterLife* discipleship materials in Indonesia while serving as the president of the Indonesian Baptist Theological Seminary. These materials have been translated into more than fifty languages and are used in more than one hundred countries. Avery led the adult-discipleship department for LifeWay Christian Resources, providing discipleship and family resources, for fifteen years. He then served ten years as senior vice president for overseas operations of the Southern Baptist Convention's International Mission Board, overseeing the work of 5,600 missionaries in 183 countries.

Avery holds a BA degree from Oklahoma Baptist University and MDiv and ThD degrees from Southwestern Baptist Theological Seminary. He has received honorary doctoral degrees from Oklahoma Baptist University and Southwest Baptist University. His writings include *MasterLife: Discipleship Training* and *MasterBuilder: Multiplying Leaders*. He is also associate editor of the *Disciple's Study Bible* and coauthor of *On Mission with God: Living God's Purpose for His Glory*; *Following Jesus: Making Disciples of Oral Learners*; *Lead Like Jesus Study*

Guide; and his most recent book written with his grandson, Matt Willis, *Learning to Soar: How to Grow Through Transitions and Trials*.

He currently lives in Arkansas with his wife, Shirley. The loves of their lives are their five children and sixteen grandchildren who are dynamic Christians, plus two young great-grandchildren.

MARK SNOWDEN has introduced thousands of missionaries and church leaders to storying. He has developed an oral Bible for an unreached people group in central Asia following his participation as project director and storyer in the *Following Jesus: Making Disciples of Oral Learners* audio series. He served as facilitator for the Lausanne Committee for World Evangelization workgroup that produced *Making Disciples of Oral Learners* as well as program director for the annual workshop of the International Orality Network. He has written for a number of publications including *Evangelical Missions Quarterly (EMQ)*, *Mission Frontiers* magazine, *Life Truths* LifeWay Sunday school curriculum, and North American Mission Board's *Church Planter Update*.

Mark presently serves as coordinator for the Strategic Planning and People Groups Team in the Church Planting Group of the North American Mission Board, SBC. He has served as a curriculum editor and consultant to the P.E.A.C.E. Plan of Saddleback Community Church in Lake Forest, California, and the overseas communications director for the International Mission Board, SBC. Mark served thirty years in Southern Baptist Convention roles including the IMB, Kentucky Baptist Convention, and Radio & TV Commission (now part of NAMB).

Mark holds a master's of science in communications management from Virginia Commonwealth University in Richmond, Virginia, and a BS degree from Eastern Kentucky University in Richmond, Kentucky. He has studied at the Southern Baptist Theological Seminary in Louisville, Kentucky, and at Georgetown College in Georgetown, Kentucky.

Mark and his wife, Mary Leigh, currently live in Alpharetta, Georgia. They have one grown daughter and one granddaughter.

Correspondence information:
Avery Willis: averywillis@sbcglobal.net
Mark Snowden: msnowden@hotmail.com

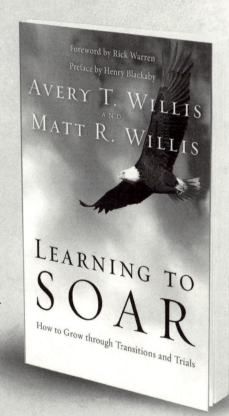